Collectible Blowtorches

Dick Sarpolus

Schiffer Publishing Ltd®

4880 Lower Valley Road, Atglen, PA 19310 USA

Foreword

This book is intended as an introduction to blowtorches - those interesting mechanical devices that have been around for a hundred years and show up today at antique malls and flea markets. For the dealer and collector/enthusiast, I have provided basic information on their uses, types, age, rarity, relative worth, restoration, etc. If you are collecting, buying, selling, trading, or just want a blowtorch for their polished brass and bronze appearance, increased knowledge about blowtorches will help you enjoy your interest. Remember - blowtorch collecting is hot! Enjoy!

In Appreciation

Thanks to my wife Lynn, her sister Janet, and Janet's husband Bob, who are so much help in the searches through flea markets and antique malls for elusive blowtorch treasures. Also, thanks to extraordinary blowtorch collector and historian Ron Carr, who confirmed that there are so many blowtorch collectors and enthusiasts out there, and who established the Blow Torch Collectors Association. Ron Carr writes, edits, and publishes "The Torch," the Newsletter of the BTCA; he's a super guy, and helped so much with this book.

Copyright © 2001 by Dick Sarpolus
Library of Congress Card Number: 00-109881

Designed by "Sue"
Type set in Korinna BT

ISBN: 0-7643-1298-7
Printed in China
1 2 3 4

Published by Schiffer Publishing Ltd.
4880 Lower Valley Road
Atglen, PA 19310
Phone: (610) 593-1777; Fax: (610) 593-2002
E-mail: Schifferbk@aol.com
Please visit our web site catalog at **www.schifferbooks.com**
We are always looking for people to write books on new and related subjects. If you have an idea for a book please contact us at the above address.

This book may be purchased from the publisher.
Include $3.95 for shipping.
Please try your bookstore first.
You may write for a free catalog.

In Europe, Schiffer books are distributed by
Bushwood Books
6 Marksbury Ave.
Kew Gardens
Surrey TW9 4JF England
Phone: 44 (0) 20 8392-8585; Fax: 44 (0) 20 8392-9876
E-mail: Bushwd@aol.com
Free postage in the U.K., Europe; air mail at cost.

Contents

Most people would recognize these items as blowtorches even if they know nothing about them. This larger torch by Clayton & Lambert and the smaller one by Lenk Mfg. are typical of those seen at many antique shops, antique malls, and flea markets. Cleaned and polished, they make interesting, decorative pieces.

In almost every antique mall, flea market, and collectible shop I've ever been in, I've seen at least a few old blowtorches. It seems that if it's old and made of brass, it's assumed to be of interest and therefore worth something. The dealers I've talked to about blowtorches say that sooner or later, they sell; so somebody out there appreciates them. As I've gotten into the hobby of collecting blowtorches myself and learned more about them, I've found that there are a surprising number of active collectors, searching for these elusive objects.

Some people have hundreds of torches and some stop after a few, using them as interesting accent pieces and decorations. I've seen them used as a unique wall display in homes, cocktail bars, and restaurants. In our home, my wife and I have arranged almost 100 blowtorches in different areas of our living room; we enjoy the appearance of these unique tools. Some collectors display them on shelves or in bookcases in their den, or squirrel them away in boxes in the basement or garage. Before we get too deep into the collecting mystique, let's define just what these items are.

Blowtorches have been around since the late 1800s, about as long as gasoline, the most common blowtorch fuel, has been available. I've seen an 1895 tool catalog, with a number of blowtorches offered. The oldest patent date on an actual blowtorch that I have in my collection is 1890. I've seen blowtorch patents as old as 1882. The Otto Bernz Company, one of the early blowtorch manufacturers, was established in 1876, and blowtorches were among their earliest products. Blowtorches are tools, and so were made to perform certain functional jobs.

Here's a list of many of the blowtorch uses that these products were made for, as have been mentioned in torch ads, catalogs, patents, etc.

Asphalt floor laying, softening asphalt	Preheating engine cylinders
Barrel making	Preheating items to be soldered
Bending metal rod and pipe	Rain gutter installation and repair
Branding cattle, logs, telephone and power poles	Repairing jewelry
Brazing bicycle and motorcycle frames	Softening glass for blowing
Burning off unwanted brush	Soldering wire, cable, connectors
Burning off paint, softening paint to be scraped off	Soldering pipes
Destroying yellow jackets and hornets	Soldering bicycle spokes
Emergency lighting	Starting back fires, forest service
Heating liquids	Starting hard coal
Heating rivets	Straightening auto parts
Heating soldering irons	Tempering tools
Heating water-jacketed glue pots	Thawing pipes
Loosening rusted bolts, nuts, or parts	Thawing railroad switches
Melting lead for bullet or toy casting	Welding
Melting metals	Thawing or warming engine blocks

Along with the list of jobs that blowtorches were used for, we can list the types of people that would be using the torches:

Assayers	Jewelers	Plumbers
Chemists	Laboratory Workers	Public Utility Workers
Dentists	Linesmen	Radio Workers
Electricians	Loggers	Ranchers
Farmers	Mechanics	Repairmen
Glass Blowers	Opticians	Roofers
Hobbyists	Painters	Sheet Metal Workers

No wonder a large number of blowtorches can still be found today; they were used for so many purposes. Through ads and catalogs, we know that blowtorches were made up through the 1950s and even into the 1960s. They finally went out of production in this country due to the availability of disposable propane tanks which could be had with easily attached and simple-to-use torch fittings; much safer and trouble-free as compared to gasoline-fueled blowtorches. Electric soldering irons and sol-dering guns also made it easier and safer to do many soldering jobs. New composite materials, plastics, new adhesives, and new electric welding equipment all combined to eliminate the need for blowtorches. Even with all the modern alternatives, it's interesting to note that some gasoline blowtorches are still produced today in countries outside the U.S. How many items can you think of that are still produced in essentially the same form more than 100 years since their introduction?

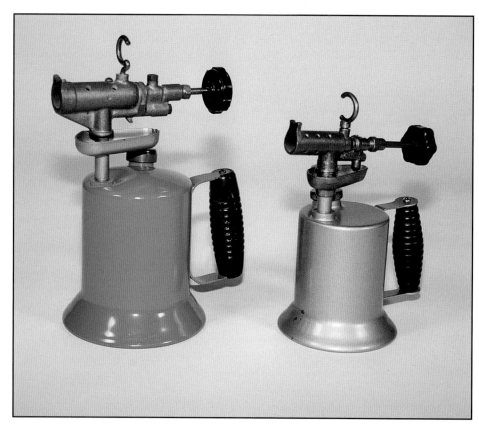

These steel tank torches are examples made in the 1950s or possibly 1960s. Steel was used for the tanks rather than brass to lower the manufacturing cost. Gasoline blowtorch manufacture and sale in the U.S. ceased during the 1960s.

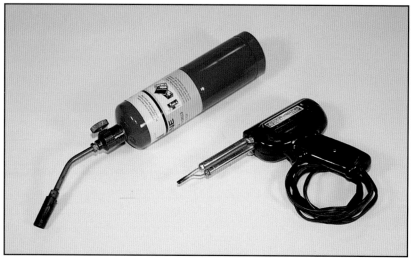

Two of the products responsible for ending the usage of blowtorches: the disposable propane tank torch and the electric soldering gun. Far safer than the old gasoline or alcohol blowtorches.

One of the most common uses of a blowtorch is for soldering jobs. This shows how the soldering iron was positioned with the hook on top of most torches to hold the copper soldering tip in the torch's flame so it can be heated and used.

It takes more than just the age of an item to make people want to collect it. In the case of blowtorches, I'd say several factors contribute to make them of interest. The basic material used in their construction, brass for the tanks and bronze for the burners, simply doesn't rust and resists corrosion over the years. Most amazingly, even when the brass and bronze parts are up to a hundred years old, they can still be cleaned, brushed, and buffed to a high shine that results in an attractive display item; they look as good or better than when they were first produced. Polished brass looks almost like gold! A cleaned and polished blowtorch is just a good-looking thing!

Another attraction to the mechanically inclined is the variety of designs found in blowtorches. They had one purpose; to produce a flame and heat, to accomplish different tasks. Those who designed and built them used their own ingenuity to get the job done; they came up with the ideas, they patented what they thought was the best way to do the job, and they started companies to produce and sell the blowtorches they had designed. Collecting and studying the torches, you can see how the construction techniques changed over the years, going from hand crafted and complex assemblies with decorative touches to simplified mass production designs. The changes in blowtorch design and construction parallels the changes and increased capabilities of the American industrial companies.

Two examples of the unique and interesting blowtorches made in the early part of the 20th century. Their appearance and history make them of interest to collectors and historians today. On the left is an early Turner with the pump in the handle and an unusual burner design, and on the right a Bernz torch having a cast brass tank and a patent date of 1910.

Blowtorches offer a real challenge to the collector - they were first produced well over one hundred years ago so would be expected to be fairly scarce today. But, due to their construction materials, many have survived the years intact and they can be cleaned up to a very good appearance. They were produced by more than one hundred different companies, with many different designs appearing over the years, so there are potentially a real variety of torches out there to be discovered and acquired. And there is information available, in the form of advertisements, catalogs, patents, etc., so that with enough searching, the torches can be identified and dated - something important to any collector. Collectible blowtorches are out there, some yet to be removed from cellar workshops, barns, attics, factories, or garages. Some show up at flea markets, antique malls and shops, or garage sales. And there are other collectors already out there, around the world, buying, selling, and trading. Pick one up for fun, or get hooked and you'll be a real blowtorch collector; it's the "hot" collectible.

Chapter Two

How Old, How Rare Are They?

The blowtorch on the left is one of the earliest made; its patent date is 1890 and the manufacturer was the Union Heater Supply Company. Note the intricate decorative design and more complex construction compared with the torch on the right, a much later Sears & Roebuck item. The Sears blowtorch was engineered to be as simple and low cost as possible to produce. This example was likely made in the 1950s or 1960s.

Like any collectible item, it helps if you're buying or selling to know as much as possible about the piece. Is it common, or rare? Is it old, newer, or really old? Is it complete, missing parts, or made up of mismatched parts? Is it in good condition, restorable, or corroded beyond saving and good only as a source for parts to complete other torches? Is it made of brass and bronze and likely worth more, or made of steel and probably worth less?

With the experience of a growing collection, the enthusiast learns some of the answers to these questions; usually learning the hard way and paying more than he should for a common item, or passing up that rare find because of not knowing or not recognizing what it really was. That's all part of the collecting game. I hope I can make it a little easier by providing some basic and helpful information about blowtorches.

Knowledge is the key to identifying the item, and the more information in the form of literature about blowtorches the better we can determine how old it may be. One quick and easy indication of the age is the patent date frequently cast or stamped into a torch. When I see a pre-1900 patent date, I know the torch is most likely really an old one. A patent date does not tell you when the item was actually made, only when the design was patented; so the torch could have been produced ten or twenty or more years after the patent was issued or applied for. And an early patent date doesn't necessarily mean that the blowtorch is rare and valuable; in the early 1900s there were a lot of blowtorches produced by high volume factories with many of them having survived until today. More common torches, that are easier to find, should be priced

lower; likewise, the rarer, hard to find types should be more expensive, even regardless of age.

But, this can only be the case when the sellers are aware of the difference in the torches. As blowtorch collecting is not yet a widespread hobby and reference material about blowtorches has not been generally available, the prices usually asked for torches have had very little to do with the actual rarity of the piece. That won't change until and unless those selling the torches learn more about them, and then only if a real demand develops for them. Although torches have been around for a hundred years, the collecting of them as a recognized activity is in its infancy; we're getting in at the ground floor of the hobby.

We know the first blowtorches were produced about twenty years before the turn of the century and they were pretty well phased out by 1970 at the very latest in the United States; some production continues today in other countries. That means any torches we find will probably be at least thirty years old and could be as much as one hundred-twenty years old; that's a wide spread. There are some generalizations that can be made to get the approximate age of a blowtorch, but of course there are always exceptions to any "rules" and those exceptions can cause you collecting trouble. Even so, I'll take a shot at some general ways you may be able to roughly date a torch if there's no patent date on the item and you have no definite catalog or other information.

Some of the oldest blowtorches have no pump for pressurizing the fuel inside, and the fuel tank was frequently made from a machined casting rather than drawn from sheet metal.

This very old blowtorch is a Clayton & Lambert No. 8 from the early 1900s. It does not have an air pump and the small tank is made from a brass casting.

Earlier torches have the pressurizing pump made as part of the handle for holding the entire blowtorch; later models have the pump mounted on the top of the tank, with a separate, simpler handle for the whole torch.

The blowtorch on the left has the air pump built as part of the handle, while the torch on the right has a less costly arrangement with a simple handle attachment and the pump mounted on the tank.

Early torches do not have provisions for holding a soldering iron on top of the torch with the iron's copper tip positioned in the torch's flame to heat it. Later models had steel clamp-on arrangements to hold the soldering iron, and some had the top hooks cast-in as part of the burner. Newer torches had separately cast hooks that threaded into holes drilled and tapped in the top of the burner assembly.

The older Schaefer & Beyer blowtorch on the left has soldering iron brackets clamped around the burner, while the newer torch on the right has its soldering iron hook made separately and screwed into a tapped hole in the burner.

Earlier torches with the pump in the handle had additional control valves on that pump assembly; later models were simpler, with no additional control valve.

This older blowtorch with its pump in the handle has an additional adjusting valve on the bottom of the pump. This feature was eliminated on later model torches.

On the torches with wooden handles, older models had more complexly shaped handles; newer models had simpler and presumably cheaper, easier to manufacture handles.

Older torches had fancier handle brackets; cast and machined, possibly threaded into the tank. Newer torches had lower cost brackets, maybe a stamped steel bracket.

The older Clayton & Lambert blowtorch on the left has separately cast and machined handle brackets screwed into tapped fittings on the tank; the newer Bernz torch on the right has a simple formed steel bracket for the handle, and the bracket is soldered to the tank.

The earliest torches had wooden handles on the main control valve; later torches had cast iron or in a few cases, cast brass control valve handles. Newer torches have cast Bakelite control valve handles.

The older Clayton & Lambert blowtorch on the left has a small wooden handle on the main control valve, and the newer Ashton torch on the right has a cast iron control knob. Manufacturers later went to cast Bakelite or plastic control knobs.

Earlier blowtorches had filler plugs in dished tank bottoms, to make it easier to fill them with gasoline. Late models eliminated the bottom filler plug, saving cost, and requiring removal of the pump to add the fuel.

In the bottom of this older and/or more expensive blowtorch is a removable plug for pouring in the gasoline. Later, lower cost torches required that the pump be removed to put the fuel in the tank.

Later torches were made with steel rather than brass fuel tanks. They were lower in cost, but the steel was much more susceptible to rust and corrosion.

Older torches may have the manufacturer's name embossed into the top or bottom of the tank; later models may have the manufacturer's name stamped into the tank and/or cast into the burner; the newer models were most likely identified with decals or stick-on labels, which may be gone by the time you come across the torch.

Note the complexity of the burner assembly on the older blowtorch at the left, as compared to the simpler and lower cost burner on the newer Turner torch at the right.

Older burners tend to be simpler in design; later models had complex castings and/or were made up of multiple parts, presumably for better performance. This was possible as manufacturing techniques developed and improved. The newest torches were again going to the simplest possible castings and designs.

General appearance is not an indication of age; a heavily blackened torch has been used a lot, and a badly corroded torch has been subjected to harmful environmental conditions. Neither will tell how old the torch is.

In general, the newest blowtorches had design and construction features which were simpler to mass-produce, resulting in a lower cost product. Older torches often had interesting, more complex designs; double control valves, complicated burner shapes and internal passages, etc. The designs might have performed well, but they would certainly cost more to produce. The older units may even have had features for novel or interesting styling; all the emphasis was not on low cost.

This blowtorch by the Detroit Torch Mfg. Co. is very dirty, with blackened deposits on the burner indicating past use and corrosion on the brass tank indicating storage under adverse conditions. Neither of these things gives any indication of the actual age of this torch.

Chapter Three
Blowtorches and Their Variations

There are blowtorches in a diversity of types, styles, and sizes - and there are blowtorch variations, which the blowtorch collector may or may not want to have in his collection. Any collector has to draw the line somewhere, and going after too much diversity can dilute your effort and interest, not to mention costing more. Let's talk about the "standard" blowtorch first, then get a bit into the variations. I think we can define "blowtorch" as a "device which burns gasoline to produce a flame, and intense heat, used for various tasks such as soldering and paint removal." Blowtorches are recognized without prompting by most people even if they've never seen one before; they sort of look like what they are. They've been used in movies; one of the Marx brothers used a blowtorch to light his cigar in one of their famous comedy films. More recently in a Batman movie, the bad guy, Two Face, used a blowtorch to light his cigar or cigarette. And blowtorches show up in cartoons or in comic strips occasionally.

Here are three blowtorches, all having the same basic parts operating in the same manner, but just look at the design variation between them. The large number of different blowtorch configurations is one of the things that intrigue collectors.

The most prominent thing first noticed about a blowtorch probably is that it is made primarily of brass and can be cleaned and polished up to be an attractive display item. That's likely why so many blowtorches show up at antique markets; there apparently is an unwritten rule that if it's old and made of brass, it must be valuable. Even if it is really dirty, dealers will indicate on their price tag that the item is made of brass and can be cleaned up; or they may polish a small area to show the potential. Some collectors limit their interest only to brass-tanked blowtorches, but I feel there are quite a lot of very interesting torches with steel construction, both steel tanks and cast iron burners. That's up to the collector.

The polished brass Ashton blowtorch on the left certainly looks good; the painted steel tanked blowtorch on the right may not appeal to all collectors, but note its unique shape and design layout.

A blowtorch has a cylindrical tank to contain the gasoline fuel, a handle so you can hold and use the torch, a burner on top with a control valve knob to regulate the flame produced, a priming cup to pre-heat the burner, possibly a hook on top to position a soldering iron, and, usually, a pump to pressurize the fuel tank. The pump may be in the handle or directly on the tank; the burner is shaped differently depending on the manufacturer's design ideas. There may be more or fewer control knobs depending on the complexity of a particular design.

Blowtorches came in different sizes, or tank capacities; the most common is referred to as the quart size. Obviously, the tank capacity is about one quart. There are smaller size tanks, referred to as the pint size. And a very few with larger tanks, referred to as the gallon size, although they don't really contain a full gallon. Pint size torches are fairly common and seem to have been made by all the larger manufacturers. The larger, gallon-type is quite rare; I've only seen a few in many years of collecting. I think the gallon size is simply too large, and would be too heavy, for the average person to actually use.

These three blowtorches show the relationship of the three common sizes torches were produced in; gallon, quart, and pint. The large size is very rarely seen; the quart size is the standard, and the pint size torches are found occasionally.

The pint sized tanks are approximately 3 1/4" in diameter and 5" high. The standard quart size tanks are about 4" in diameter and 5 1/2" high, and the so-called gallon size tanks are roughly 5 1/2" in diameter and 6" high.

Another variable is the actual shape of the fuel tank. In addition to the pint, quart, or gallon size, torches were made with a flattened, narrow tank style, referred to as the "auto" torch. These auto torches were made with a narrow tank so they could be used in confined spaces, such as on an automobile. With their different shape, they are desirable and a nice addition to any collection.

Here are three examples of "auto" torches, so called because they were intended for use on automobiles and their narrow shape would permit them to fit in restricted areas. Left to right, these three examples are by Bernz, Wall, and Turner.

One of the main uses of a blowtorch is to heat up a soldering iron for soldering work; torches can also heat up a branding iron for use on wooden boxes or furniture, and maybe even for branding cattle. Special type torches were made with the branding iron held in place ahead of the output flame, and some have a soldering iron positioned ahead of the flame. The soldering iron types may have the brass fuel container within a Bakelite cylinder/handle assembly. I prize these unusual configuration torches and have several in my collection.

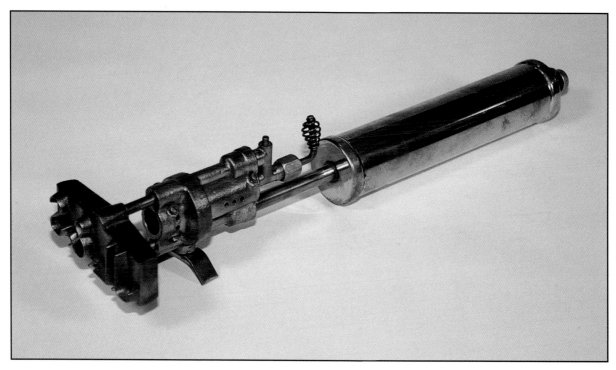

This blowtorch, in a horizontal cylinder layout, has a branding iron positioned ahead of the flame for this specialized use.

16

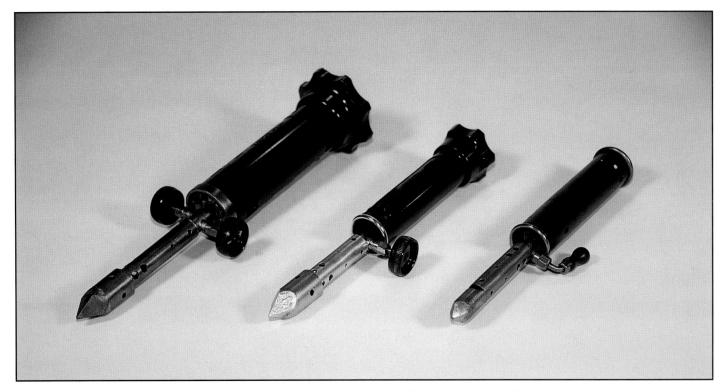

These soldering torches have the same basic blowtorch features, a fuel tank and preheating cup, and also have a copper soldering point mounted ahead of the torch flame. They're a special purpose design for soldering work. The Bakelite handle encloses the fuel tank. All three were made by Justrite.

In addition to the conventional type torches described above, you'll most likely run across several varieties of similar devices, and will have to decide if you want to collect any of them also. By these, I mean the dual-cylinder alcohol torches, the alcohol or gasoline blow-pipe torches, the jewelers' torches, the pistol grip soldering torches, or the miniature torches, usually alcohol-fueled. All of these types were intended for much lighter duty soldering work than the conventional blowtorch; they're more of a hobby item, not a real working tool. Probably the largest manufacturer of these devices was the Lenk Manufacturing Company of Boston, Massachusetts, and they made all of the different types. They are fairly common and so have lower price tags than the larger, heavier standard blowtorches. Some of the alcohol torch variations are quite rare and, of course, they are considerably more valuable.

I have enough of these "special" types in my overall collection to represent a cross-section of the general ones that were made, and I like them as they offer a sub-type, a real variation to the standard torches. They are also much smaller, take up less space, and I can display about two dozen of the mini types on one fairly small bookshelf. The branding iron, paint scraper, and soldering iron types are larger and I mix them in with the other blowtorches. There is also a fairly modern blowtorch variation intended to burn cactus and other ground vegetation; not a good looking device, but interesting for part of a collection.

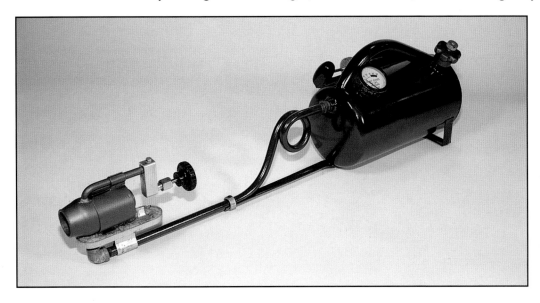

This most unusual blowtorch with a large capacity fuel tank and extended burner position is specifically designed for use in burning off unwanted ground vegetation. It has been used in forest fire fighting situations.

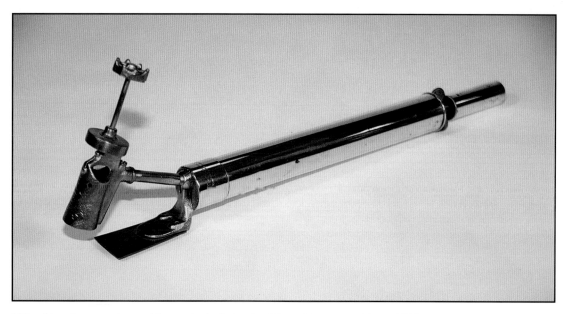

This old and extremely rare blowtorch made by the Climax Company with an 1898 patent date has a built-in paint scraper blade below the burner flame. An unusual configuration intended solely for paint removal, one of the most popular early uses of a blowtorch.

The dual-tube alcohol torches offered small size, lightweight, smaller flame, easy start-up and operation (no pressurization) and the use of a somewhat safer fuel; usually denatured alcohol was recommended. They were also referred to as self-generating alcohol blowtorches. Describing the most common arrangement, one of the two tubes had a right angle nozzle coming out of the tube top; that was the actual soldering torch. The other tube, the priming tube, contained a wick under the re-movable top, which was lit and the flame used to pre-heat the nozzle of the first tube. Heated enough, the alcohol in the main tube would gas off through the output nozzle and could then be lit; the result was a hot, pointed flame. The priming tube was then extinguished, and was no longer needed. The flame was then self-generating with no further priming required. I have never had any desire to try to actually light up any of these torches; seems a bit dangerous to me.

Four examples of the two-tube or dual-cylinder alcohol torch, apparently quite popular with a lot of them available today. Left to right, by Dunlap, Waltock, unknown, and R.L. Livingston.

These dual-cylinder alcohol torches are usually about 1" in diameter and 5" long, with a sheet metal clip holding the two tubes together for convenience and storage. Earlier versions are typically made of brass, with later ones being nickel- or chrome-plated. Many of those I've seen appear to have been used very little if at all. With so many of the two tube torches available, unless one is of an unusual configuration they are usually fairly low priced.

The blow pipe torches are typically about 2" in diameter and 6" high, some made with a cast base probably for stability. They have a removable cap over the top 3/4" diameter outlet, and a wick in the outlet where the alcohol is lit. Positioned alongside the flame's position is a small brass tube with a small outlet hole at right angles to the flame; the tube is mounted to the side of the cylinder and is adjustable vertically. Connected to the bottom of the tube is a length of rubber hose; by blowing through the hose when the torch is burning, the blast of air going through the flame will produce a blast of pointed flame at right angle to the cylinder, and that flame can be used for soldering. Advertisements claim a much fiercer fire than can be obtained in any other way.

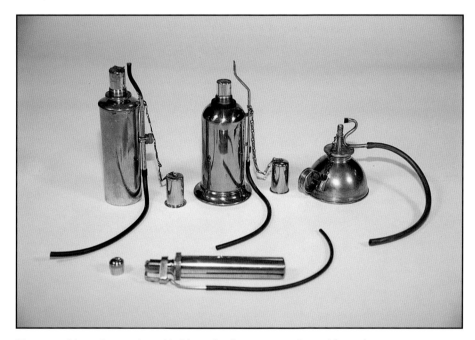

These are blow-pipe torches. Air, blown by the operator via a rubber tube, passes at a right angle through the flame of the burning fuel and produces a directed, fine pointed flame of high heat. Intended for soldering use by jewelers and electricians.

Another variety of these mini-torches, also sized about 2" in diameter and 6" long, is the so-called jewelers' torch. These have both a right angle output nozzle, which could have a removable extension, and another tube with a wick positioned beneath the actual output nozzle, for priming. A sheet metal handle permits hand holding of this small soldering torch. None of the above-described torches have any sort of adjustable fuel feed.

These torches, usually referred to as jewelers' torches, in principle combined the two-tube torch into one item. There were usually two separate fuel chambers in the single tank.

There are also alcohol torches in several sizes which do resemble the larger blowtorches, having a burner, control valve knob, handle, and pre-heater cup beneath the burner. These can be about 2" in diameter and 3" to 6" tall, or 3" in diameter and 3" tall. Some have decals calling for alcohol fuel, some for gasoline. They appear almost toy-like, and most that I've seen for sale have been used very little.

Below:
Look at the variety of miniature blowtorches here, all made by the Lenk Company. So many have survived over the years that they are not too expensive today, except for a few rare variations.

Three examples of the miniature blowtorch. Some were made for use with gasoline, others for use with denatured alcohol as the fuel. This size torch was intended for much lighter duty than the conventional blowtorches and was not considered as a real working tool, but more as a home hobby item. This type of small blowtorch was made by Lenk, Turner, Dunlap, and Fulton.

The pistol grip alcohol torches resemble today's electric soldering guns, but rather than an electric mechanism they contain a tank for the alcohol fuel, with an output nozzle for the soldering flame. The front of the tank, around the output nozzle, is concave. With the torch held so the tank is vertical, that cavity can be filled with alcohol and lit, to pre-heat or prime the output nozzle. I'd guess these devices were produced in the 1940s or 50s, and it certainly appears the electric soldering gun would be much safer.

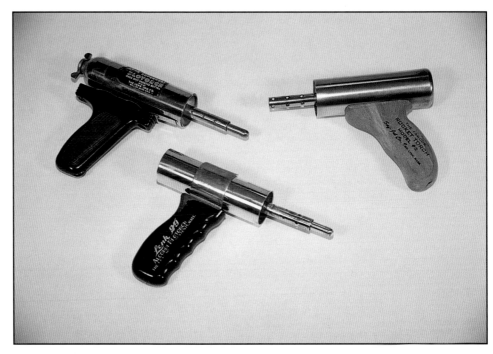

Here are three pistol grip gun-type soldering torches. They were held with the tip pointed up to preheat the fuel nozzle, and then could be held like a gun for small soldering jobs. The two on the left are early and later models by Lenk and on the right is a Rocket Torch #2 by the Saf-Jet Co., Inc. All are probably from the 1950s.

One of the most interesting variations appears to be a standard blowtorch that has a heavy metal collar around the burner, with a brass tube leading down from that collar to the side of the tank, where it is soldered in position. Attached to the end of the tube is a rubber hose several feet long. This device, made by the Turner Brass Works, was listed as a Halide Refrigerant Leak Detector. In use, with the torch burning, the free end of the rubber hose was held near the joints in a charged refrigeration system. Apparently, if any of the pressurized refrigerant was leaking from a loose or bad joint, it would go through the hose to the torch and the flame would change color. Since the refrigerant was colorless, the effect on the flame's color would indicate the leaking gas. I think it's a very interesting variant in my blowtorch collection.

At first glance, this looks like a typical blowtorch, but it's not. Notice the collar around the small burner and the tube leading to a rubber hose. This is a Halide Refrigerant Leak Detector. The end of the rubber hose was held close to the joints in a refrigerant system. With the blowtorch burning, if even a small amount of refrigerant was leaking from a joint, it would travel through the tube to the burner and the flame would change color, indicating a leak.

Blowtorches have been called by many different names; when I see a listing of antique items anywhere for sale, I look for the following names:

blow torch	paint burner	hand torch
blowtorch	gasoline/gasolene torch	plumber's blowpipe
blotorch	kerosene torch	soldering iron heater
blow pipe	plumber's torch	soldering torch
brazing torch	electrician's torch	
brazing lamp	auto torch	

This is apparently a Coleman blowtorch with a unique configuration, having the burner high above the fuel tank and the handle between them. Seen like this occasionally, it may in fact be a "fake" assembled on a Coleman lantern fuel tank; still interesting for a collection.

Another product based on blowtorch construction techniques is a pressure oiler. With a typical blowtorch tank, handle, and pump, rather than a burner a device is fitted to the tank outlet with an extended nozzle and a thumb-operated trigger release. With oil in the tank and air pressure applied, release of the trigger delivers oil through the nozzle, presumably to lubricate various types of machinery. Because so little is commonly known about blowtorches, I've seen a number of these oilers advertised for sale as unusual blowtorches. Be aware that with the absence of a burner and priming cup, the item is most likely a pressure oiler and not a blowtorch but could still be an interesting, worthwhile addition to a torch collection.

This is a pressure oiler, used for lubricating any sort of machinery. Made by a blowtorch manufacturer, Huffman, utilizing the same tank, pump, and handle, but it's not any sort of blowtorch. Similar devices were made by other blowtorch manufacturers and are frequently incorrectly identified today as torches.

Chapter Four
How Blowtorches Operate and How They're Built

The principle of blowtorch operation seems deceptively simple. Gasoline is the fuel in the tank. It is pressurized to get it to the burner, and the burning gas flame is used as a heat source. In actual practice, blowtorch construction and operation is considerably more complex. For those who want to learn a bit more, we'll refer to Figure 1, the blowtorch cutaway drawing, and take you through the actual operation of this device.

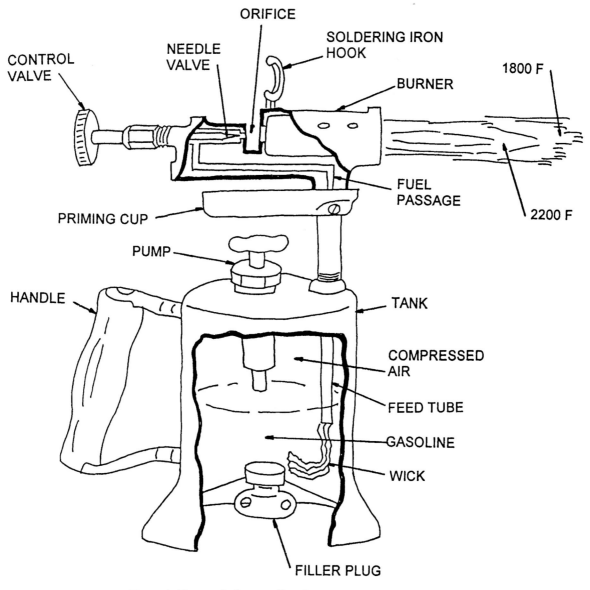

Figure 1. Blowtorch Cutaway Drawing

The gasoline in the tank is forced up to the burner through the feed pipe and fuel passage by air pressure inside the tank provided by the hand pump mounted on the tank (or in older torches, the pump is often in the handle of the torch). As the gasoline travels through the fuel passage in the burner, the heat of the burner vaporizes it while the torch is burning. When a cold torch is first started, the burner casting is pre-heated by burning liquid gasoline in the priming cup, positioned below the burner. (The priming cup looks like it is there as a drip catcher, until you understand how a torch operates.)

The gasoline vapor in the fuel passage exits through the orifice into the burner (how much fuel comes out is adjusted by the control valve) where it mixes with air and burns, resulting in a long, blue flame at the mouth of the burner. Most burners have a number of air holes to let in more air for better burning. The temperature of a blow-torch flame averages 1800 degrees F, with the hottest spot in the flame reaching 2100 to 2200 degrees F.

We illustrate the actual procedure in lighting up a blow-torch here in figures 2 through 6. Figure 2, the torch tank is filled with gasoline, but not more than 3/4 full, to leave space for the pressurized air. Most tanks are filled through a removable plug in the bottom; the dished bottom shape acts as a funnel, for easier filling. Newer, lower cost torches used a removable pump for filling the tank, to lower the manufacturing cost. Figure 3, the pump is used to pressurize air in the tank. Be sure the control valve is completely closed before pumping the air; about 20 strokes of the pump should do it.

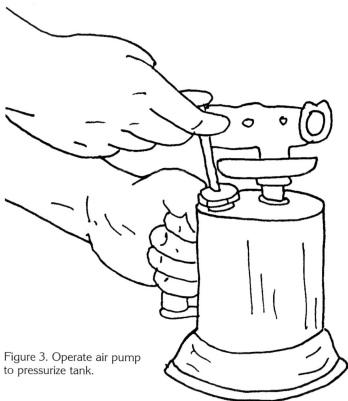

Figure 3. Operate air pump to pressurize tank.

Figure 2. Fill torch tank with gasoline through plug in bottom, not more than 3/4 full.

Figure 4, to test the fuel flow, point the nozzle into a container and open the control valve; a small stream of gasoline should spray out as the valve is opened. Figure 5, to get gasoline into the priming cup for pre-heating the burner, put one hand over the mouth of the burner and open the control valve; the gasoline will run out the lower burner holes into the priming cup. Some torches have a separate valve just for fuel flow into the priming cup. With any excess gasoline wiped off the surface of the blowtorch, light the gasoline in the priming cup so the flame will heat up the burner casting and the fuel passage inside it. Figure 6, when the fuel in the priming cup nearly all burned, open the control valve; if the torch does not light itself from the priming flame, hold a lighted match close to the heater holes or just below the nozzle. An intense blue flame should result. A yellow flame means the burner has not been sufficiently pre-heated and the torch must be turned off, allowed to cool, and pre-heated again. During operation of the torch, the air pressure in the tank can be kept up with intermittent use of the pump if necessary. The volume of the flame depends upon the control valve setting and the air pressure available.

Figure 4. Test fuel flow by pointing torch toward container and opening control valve.

Figure 5. Fill priming cup with gasoline, wipe off any excess from torch surface, and light gasoline in priming cup to pre-heat the burner.

Figure 6. With priming cup fuel mostly burned, open control valve and hold match below nozzle.

After shutting off the torch, release the air pressure in the tank and back off the control valve a bit to prevent it from jamming as the burner cools off. Considerable maintenance was needed to keep a blowtorch in good operating condition. The air pump had a leather washer as its piston which could dry out and crack, the fuel passages, needle valve, and fuel orifice could get clogged up, the upper end of the wick in the fuel pipe got charred, the packing around the control valve could leak; a lot of things to go wrong.

Warning! While I find the operation and maintenance of the blowtorch to be quite interesting to read about, **I would strongly suggest that the blowtorch collector today not try to operate these tools**; they seem quite dangerous to me. With a blowtorch 50 to 100 years old, they're not likely to be in a safe operating condition today. The average old torch likely has stuck valves, leaky gaskets and packings, leaky pumps, clogged passages, and cracked or broken parts, all making it a real hazard to try and operate. There are a few blowtorch collectors who have the know-how and ability to **completely** disassemble and rebuild an old torch to a safe (?) operating condition, and they do light 'em off. But even those collectors have stories of near-serious malfunctions, and urge others not to try and operate an old blowtorch. I'm glad of the availability of propane torches, electric soldering irons, etc., today so we don't need the gasoline-fueled blowtorches - except as collectors' items.

The materials used in the construction of a blowtorch are the reason why they can be collected today - the brass and bronze simply resists corrosion so well that even after a hundred years or more of neglect a blowtorch is still around to be found and collected. The largest part of a blowtorch is its tank, and it typically is made of sheet brass, drawn into shape. Occasionally a brass tank is found with cracks in it, destroying it for use but if it is an otherwise collectible torch, I can overlook the cracks. As torches were working tools, they may also be found dented and bent; again, I don't mind those signs of use. No matter how tarnished, the brass tanks can be buffed to a beautiful shine.

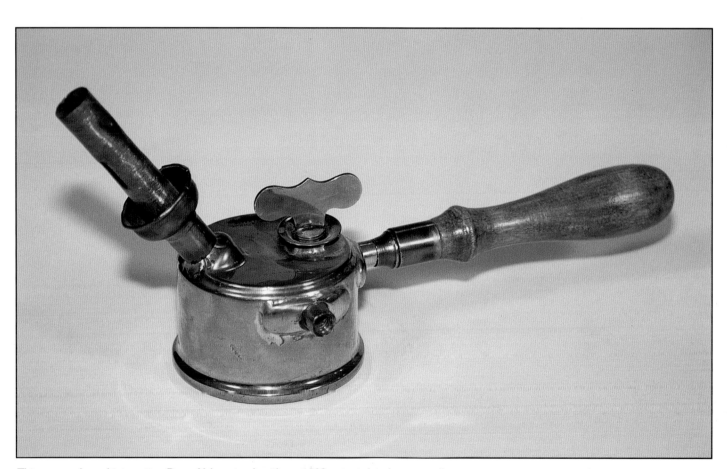

This very early and interesting Burnz Vulcan torch with an 1893 patent date has a small capacity tank, lightweight construction, no pump, and two positions for the handle.

Very old, smaller torches had heavy, thick walled tanks cast of brass or bronze; I'd imagine because technology and mass production manufacturing at that time just didn't have the capability or materials availability to make thinner, lighter tanks of sheet brass. The cast tanks are unique and they too can be cleaned and polished to a high shine.

The burners on just about all US-made blowtorches, old or newer, are made of cast bronze; the material was available, easy enough to cast and machine, withstands the high temperature of a burning blowtorch, and is extremely durable. These castings have a rough surface texture and were not smoothed and polished; wire brushing with a coarse wire wheel cleans them and restores the original as-cast appearance.

The blowtorch on the left has a typical cast bronze burner, while the Wall torch on the right has a cast iron burner. Wall is the only manufacturer known to have used cast iron burners instead of bronze.

The air pumps, whether in the torch handle or mounted directly on the tank, are usually of all brass construction except for the pump shaft, which is steel. The fittings around the control valve shaft are brass, the priming cup may be of cast brass, and the soldering iron hook and filler plug are usually cast brass or bronze. Most priming cups are made of cast iron and many of the older torches have a cast iron control valve knob. Later, Bakelite became the material of choice for the control valve knobs. Some torch manufacturers, old and newer, used cast iron for the filler plugs and upper pump fittings. Some brass tanks had steel bottoms, which I guess saved money, but in many cases the steel bottom has rusted away while the brass tank is still as good as new.

A number of later torches were made with painted steel tanks, I assume for a lower cost. Surprisingly, some brass tanks were painted, so a check with a magnet is the best way to tell for sure if a torch tank is steel or brass. Don't believe a tag in an antique shop; I've seen a number of steel tanked blowtorches for sale, and tags indicating the item is a "brass blowtorch." Some collectors want only brass torches; I think steel tanks are certainly a part of blowtorch history and some of them are very interesting and rare. I don't hesitate to add a steel tanked torch to my collection.

This Unique brand blowtorch is made with a steel tank and so must be painted. Some collectors go only for brass-tanked torches, but this unusually shaped torch is certainly a collector's item.

Some older torches had brass tanks with a steel flange around the bottom, likely for better resistance to tipping over. These torches look good with the brass tank polished and the steel lower flange nicely painted.

There are only a very few blowtorches that I know of with an aluminum tank; the Otto Bernz Co. made a torch in one year only, 1951 (all of them may have been marked with the same date, 7/51) that had a nicely shaped aluminum tank. It was certainly lighter than it would have been with steel or brass as the material, but I imagine the aluminum would have been much less durable. Bernz made the same shape torch with the conventional brass material for the tank, and a matched pair of these torches is a nice addition to a collection. The U.S. military had an aluminum-tanked blowtorch made in the 1960s, and, surprisingly, a torch patented in 1910 by the Decker Mfg. Co. had a cast aluminum tank. Except for the Bernz model, an aluminum-tanked torch is very rare.

Very few torches were made with an aluminum fuel tank; only three or four are known. On the left is a Decker torch with a 1910 patent date, in the middle a U.S. military blowtorch made by the Hunter Mfg. Co. from the 1960s, and on the right a Bernz torch from 1951, all with aluminum tanks.

I have seen a few torches, by different manufacturers, that had chrome- or nickel-plated brass tanks. The plating doesn't stand up too well under rough use, but when in good condition a chrome plated tank on a blow torch sure looks neat.

Like any consumer product made in large quantities, there were a number of manufacturers turning out blowtorches to meet the demand. One of the things I like best about collecting and working with these interesting devices is the way they demonstrate good old American ingenuity and inventiveness. They show such a variety of ideas and approaches, different designs and materials, different construction and production techniques, each the result of engineers and businessmen out to make a better product, build up their business, and make a profit. It is the American way, and it works.

I'd say the Big Four in blowtorch manufacturing were the Otto Bernz Company, the Turner Brass Works, Clayton & Lambert Co., and the P. Wall Manufacturing Co. I've seen more blowtorches made by these four companies than any others; but, another fun thing about collecting torches, there were so many other manufacturers. With inputs from many enthusiastic collectors, more than one hundred blowtorch manufacturers have been documented; and that is just in the United States. For some fun, here are a few of those we can list: Acorn Brass Works, American Products Corp., American Stove Co., Anthony Co., Ashton Manufacturing Co., Atlas Brass Works, Baum & Bender, Beach-Ross Co., Benton & Walter Mfg. Co., Best Light Co., Wm. Best Inc., Brookins Mfg. Co., Otto Bernz Co., Charles H. Besly & Co., Wm. Boekel & Co., Bolte Mfg. Co., Boston Globe Gas Light Co., L.S. Brach Mfg. Co., Bridgeport Brass Co., Carleton Co., U.S. Chaplet & Supply Co., Chausse Mfg. Co., Clayton & Lambert Co., Climax Co., Coleman Co., and the Lyon Conklin & Co. Inc. And that's only the As, Bs, and Cs!

The Otto Bernz Company was established in 1876 as a "manufacturer of plumbers tools, furnaces and torches, and mechanical specialties and small brass work" in Newark, NJ. An 1894 history book of Newark describes the Bernz company as "a branch of industry of a most useful and important character in the city of Newark is the manufacture of plumbers' tools and mechanical specialties." At that time, Bernz employed twenty workers and his factory had "modern appliances, tools, and machinery operated by a 35-horsepower steam engine."

The Bernz company stayed in Newark until the 1940s, when it relocated to Rochester, New York. In the 1950s, with a name change to BernzOmatic, the company line grew to include propane-powered outdoor appliances for camping and leisure time purposes. The emergence of small, portable propane tanks as a fuel source for plumbers' torches eliminated the need for gasoline-fueled, pressurized, hazardous blowtorches. Today, more than 100 years after the founding of the Otto Bernz Company, BernzOmatic continues in business and is a leading supplier of propane-fueled torches for a variety of uses. Quite a history, and it has made it most interesting to collect the older blowtorches made by Bernz.

An early Bernz blowtorch with a 1910 patent date, the pump in the handle, and an interesting coiled wire control knob.

Bernz, in the 1950s, made some blowtorches with a particularly gracefully shaped tank.
In 1951 they made a limited edition aluminum version in the same unique shape.

Here's a Bernz blowtorch in the large gallon size, along with one of their small pint size torches.

Three brothers named Lambert founded a company in 1882, in Ypsilanti Michigan, for the manufacture and sale of gasoline burning blowtorches. In 1887, an inventor named Clayton joined the firm with his lead melting firepot; the company was renamed Clayton & Lambert. The company relocated to Detroit in 1899 and their blowtorch and firepot business continued to grow; the company prospered. Clayton & Lambert expanded into the metal stamping business, making parts for the Detroit auto manufacturers. In World War I, C&L made parts for military applications, including blowtorches.

This early Clayton & Lambert blowtorch has no provision for soldering iron use, has a cast iron control knob, and a decorative brass handle. Notice the fuel feed tube exiting from the middle of the tank; all later torches had the fuel tube exiting the tank near the edge, opposite the handle.

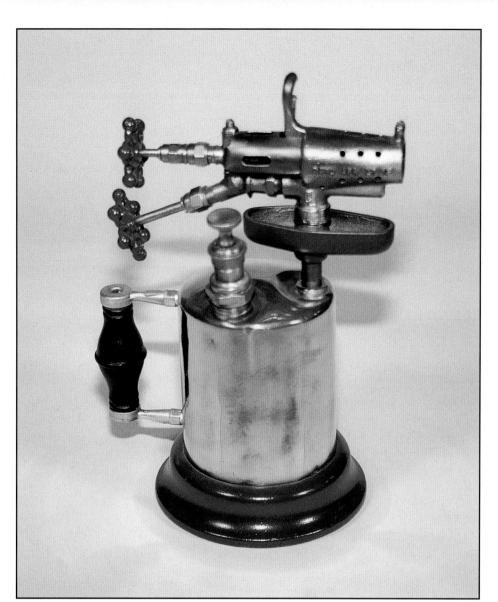

This Clayton & Lambert blowtorch shows an interesting mix of materials used; a brass fuel tank with aluminum brackets for mounting the handle and a steel lower flange around the tank. This particular piece also has a complex burner with two control valves, both with cast iron knobs.

A nice pint size C&L blowtorch with a wooden handle on the control valve, pump in the handle, and an additional valve on the bottom of the pump.

The blowtorch business continued through the depression years, and during World War II C&L developed a process for the manufacture of steel cartridge cases, employing thousands of workers making many millions of the cartridge cases. After the war, C&L moved their blowtorch manufacturing from Detroit to Louisville, Kentucky, and, later, to Buckner, Kentucky. A blowtorch variation developed for the government was a special flat tank torch to fit in a government tool kit. Clayton & Lambert continued to build their torches until 1970; by that time, the demand for gasoline blowtorches had simply stopped.

E.S. Turner started a company in 1871, sold it to other owners in 1880, and the firm incorporated as The Turner Brass Works. They specialized in gasoline, kerosene, and alcohol torches, furnaces, and automobile accessories for many years. In 1904, Turner acquired the White Mfg. Co., also a blowtorch maker, and for some time made blowtorches under the Turner-White name. In 1907 they built a new factory with an area of 60,000 square feet in Sycamore Illinois, and in their 1916 product catalog they claimed to be the largest concern in the world engaged in the manufacture of torches, furnaces (fire pots) and brazers. Turner was acquired by Bernz-O-Matic after the 1960's, and later a tool company bought the Sycamore, Illinois, plant; in 1999 that plant was closed down.

This early Turner blowtorch has the pump in the handle and an unusual short burner with two control knobs.

34

Several manufacturers produced blowtorches with chrome-plated fuel tanks such as this pint sized Turner, which also has complex, decorative handle, mounts.

This Turner Baffle model blowtorch patented in 1920 has a unique horizontally placed pump with the wooden handle positioned down from the pump.

The label of the P. Wall Manufacturing Company, Grove City, Pennsylvania, says "superior products since 1864." They have been around a long time, but I haven't yet come across any older Wall blowtorches. Most of the Wall torches I've seen have had steel tanks rather than brass. There is an interesting variety of Wall torches, with different tanks, styles, etc. Wall is about the only manufacturer I know of that had several models with cast iron, rather than cast bronze, burners; interesting. I was inspecting a Wall blowtorch at an antique market, and a passerby struck up a conversation about her many years working at Wall, how they were a leading blowtorch manufacturer, and what a great place it was to work.

A most unusual auto torch by Wall with the burner low down in front of the tank and at a right angle to it. Apparently made for some specific use.

This Wall Dreadnaught blowtorch has a steel tank and an unusual handle and pump arrangement.

36

Two Wall blowtorches, showing their use of a cast iron burner. Wall is the only torch manufacturer known to use cast iron rather than bronze for their burner construction.

The Lenk Manufacturing Company, Boston, Massachusetts, although they produced primarily the smaller, hobby-type alcohol torches, would have to be included as one of the highest volume blowtorch manufacturers. The small Lenk torches are seen frequently at antique flea markets and malls. Lenk produced many, many different models of their basic designs; different sized tanks, different attachments, handles, priming cups, wind shields, etc., along with jewelers torches and two tube alcohol torches. Acquiring only Lenk torches could result in a fairly large, interesting collection.

Two typical Lenk mini size torches in two sizes, made in versions for either alcohol or gasoline fuel.

A Lenk jewelers' torch on the left along with a Lenk two tube alcohol torch.

I consider this an extremely rare collectible Lenk mini torch, their only model having a pump. In more than ten years of collecting, this is only the second one I've seen.

Knowing some of the histories such as these about the various blowtorch manufacturers make the collecting of their products even more interesting. The search for information about the manufacturers can be as consuming as the search for their products; company publications, catalogs, and ads are a help to the collector in identifying and dating their acquisitions.

Chapter Six
Foreign Blowtorches

It should be no surprise that blowtorches were made in other countries in addition to the United States. It appears that at least some were imported into the U.S., likely in the 1930s through the 1950s, judging by the torches I've come across in our antiquing. I've seen blowtorches, in fairly small numbers, made in England, Germany, and Sweden. Enough similar torches showing up in our flea markets and antique malls probably means they were commercially available in the U.S. at one time. However, they are scarce enough that you're not going to find very many foreign-made blowtorches to add to a collection.

Foreign blowtorches are also made in various sizes, as these three British torches show. I'd guess their capacities at a quart, pint, and half pint. Left to right, these torches were made by Governor, Chas. Twigg, and Monitor.

The foreign torches are usually different enough in appearance and construction to be noticed, if you're a blowtorch enthusiast. Close inspection may reveal the manufacturer's name and country of origin, possibly even some instructions for the torch's use, stamped into the brass. I've seen a number of German torches made by G. Barthel and Swedish torches by Radius. We don't know what formal arrangements were in place for these and/or other foreign made torches to be imported and sold here in the U.S.

Every overseas torch I have does not have a wooden handle, unlike so many of the U.S.-made blowtorches. The metal handles on the foreign torches are frequently made of perforated steel, rolled into a round or flattened oval shape. And rather than the U.S.-typical cast bronze burners, many of my foreign torches have a burner made up of bent tubing with a sheet brass outer cover or with the steel tubing around a brass center burner. Again, these comments are based on my fairly limited experience with the foreign-made blowtorches. Acquiring foreign torches is a tough challenge, unless you're fortunate enough to be able to spend some time abroad, looking for second-hand treasures.

Rather than by being lucky enough to find a foreign-made torch at a flea market or antique mall, another way of adding foreign blowtorches to your collection is by trading with a torch collector in another country. I learned of a French collector through the Blow Torch Collectors Association. This particular collector is a real enthusiast, having more than 800 torches. I sent him a letter, with photos of about a dozen of my "doubles" which I would be willing to trade. He responded, with copies of ads depicting a number of French and Swedish torches. He had selected nine of my torches he wished to trade for. I picked an equal number of torches from his offering, responded with a letter, and packed up my nine blowtorches for shipment to France. Within a few weeks, I was pleased to receive a box containing nine new additions to my collection, all from France and Sweden. A good trade.

This French blowtorch, made by Vesta from 1920 to 1934, shows why I like some of the foreign models. Note the unusual burner arrangement with the tightly bent steel tube fuel line around the burner to pre-heat the fuel, and the brass pump in the handle covered by a perforated steel piece.

These two neat blowtorches are from France and Sweden; both small torches do not
have pumps and have steel handles. The French model on the left was made by Rippes
between 1935 and 1950; the Swedish model on the right, by Max Sievert, Stockholm.

These two German blowtorches, although very different, were both made by G. Barthel. The large
torch is an interesting gasoline model with the pump in the tank at an angle above the metal
handle. The handle also serves as a storage compartment. The small torch is an alcohol type.

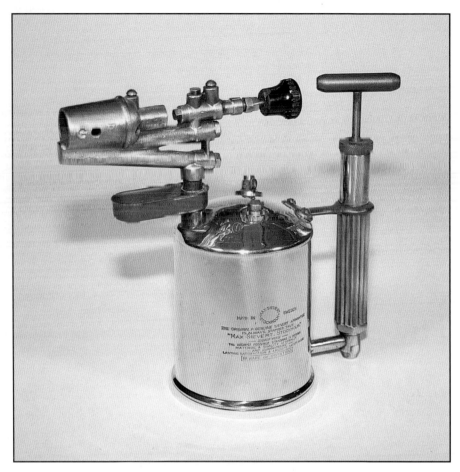

I don't know the age of this Swedish torch by Max Sievert, but I'd guess it was older because of the pump in the handle.

Below:
A really wild one. This blowtorch was apparently designed primarily for soldering, with its removable soldering iron tip positioned ahead of the flame. This torch was made by Primus in Norway, and I bought it from a dealer in Australia.

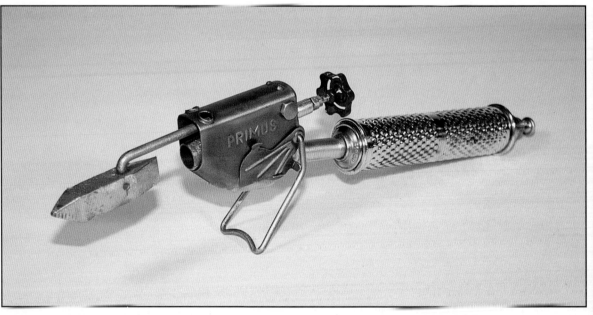

Today's Internet on-line auctions permit us to do collecting on a more global basis. I've seen blowtorches for sale from Canada, England, Australia, New Zealand, and Peru and I'm sure sellers from other countries will be showing up. It is pretty easy to buy through the on-line auctions and this can make our torch collections have more of an international representation.

Regarding the cost of foreign blowtorches, the common styles seem to sell for a bit more than the common US-made torches but the rare and unique foreign torches don't get up to the high prices paid for rare and unique US-made torches. Maybe we collectors in the U.S. simply prize the U.S.-made torches more than the foreign torches that are less familiar to us.

Chapter Seven
How to Clean, Restore, and Repair Blowtorches

The usual advice for any older antique or collectible item is not to attempt to refinish it for a better appearance, unless it is really, really bad. With age, most metal items acquire a patina that can't be duplicated and can enhance its appearance as an older treasure. That may be true for many things, but it's not, I believe, true for blowtorches. A blowtorch is a tool, and when it was used, gasoline was burning; soot was being formed and deposited on the surfaces, and the heat was affecting the color and appearance of the metal parts. After that, the blowtorch may have been stored in a barn, cellar, or even outdoors for fifty years or more, subject to the effects of weather. The brass and bronze parts remain beneath the surface changes, but most old, used blowtorches have a pretty disreputable appearance and would not be welcome for display in today's homes.

Which one would you want to display in your living room? Although some collectors keep their torch treasures in as-found condition, I believe in cleaning and polishing them for the best possible appearance.

Antiquers today recognize that older brass, bronze, and copper items can be cleaned and polished to look almost like gold. That's exactly what is done to many old blowtorches before they're put out for sale in an antique shop, at a high price. Unfortunately for the blowtorch collector, the polishing can and frequently is overdone so the "refinished" appearance does not resemble the original appearance of this tool. I prefer to clean and polish the parts, and I'll describe just how I do it, so the "restored" torches look as good as they did when first manufactured, but not too much better. I make no attempt to try to get the torches into true working condition; that is, I don't worry if the pump doesn't actually develop air pressure, if the seals on the fuel connections are actually air tight, if the fuel passages are clear, or if the wicks are in place for the fuel supply. These things will never be lit off again; from now on, they're display pieces, not working tools.

First step is to do some basic disassembly so the parts will be easier to work on. The wooden handles, usually held in place with screws, are removed for stripping and repainting. The pump assemblies are removed from the tank or handle, and the burner itself is unscrewed from the tank. Some burners can be further broken down, but it's usually not necessary to do that to clean them up. The control valve can be unscrewed from the burner, the priming cup removed, the soldering iron hook unscrewed, and the filler plug removed. If there is a wind shield in place, I usually remove it and throw it away. That may be upsetting to a collector who wants everything authentic, but I feel the steel shields hide the interesting burner parts and styles from view, so prefer to not have them on most of the "completed for display" blowtorches.

Left:
The start of a restoration project is this older pump in handle model blowtorch by the Detroit Torch Mfg. Co. with a patent date of 1918. There are no missing parts, no major dents or scratches, but the brass is really stained and corroded; this torch may have been sitting in a barn or cellar for 75 years. The first step is to disassemble it as much as possible.

This much disassembly will allow us to clean and polish all the parts and put the torch back together. I used a pipe wrench to unscrew the burner from the tank, and the usual wrenches and screwdrivers for everything else. I couldn't get the pump tube out of its brackets because it was soldered to the bottom fitting, but that won't prevent a good cleaning and polishing.

All the parts look a lot better after some wire brushing and polishing. The buffing wheel doesn't do it all, as some handwork is needed around the pump and its mounting brackets. The cast iron parts will be primed and painted before reassembly.

How about that! The old Detroit torch looks good enough now, probably better than when it was brand new, to be displayed in our living room.

Some basic tools are needed for disassembly; adjustable wrenches, screwdrivers, probably a pipe wrench, and a large, secure bench vise will do in most cases. Although it might be possible to clean up a blowtorch by hand with a wire brush and even polish it by hand, it would be a very laborious job; I've never done it. I consider an electric bench-mounted buffer/polisher, which will also accept a wire brush, a real necessity for cleaning up these blowtorches. My first such tool was a Sears Craftsman Bench Grinder, 6" wheels and 1/3 horsepower. To speed up the work, I then went for a Sears 8", one full horsepower model which I now consider the minimum sufficient if you're go-ing to do much of this work. Automotive tool supply out-fits such as Eastwood offer special buffer motors and floor stands, in the $600 range for a full buffing setup. I've found that a bench grinder, with the wheels removed and replaced with buffs and wire brushes, is much less costly and works very well. I bolt the bench grinder firmly to a solid workbench. I've rarely used the grinding wheels that came with these tools, replacing them with buffs and wire brushes of various densities. I use 6" buffs and 5" or 6" wire brushes. I've found that cheap wire brushes don't last too long, with the individual wire bristles eventually loos-ening and flying out. I now use the highest quality brushes I can find, and sometimes use the heavy duty twisted wire bundle type, sold at welding supply shops; they're quite a bit more expensive and may be too rough for all work, but they last much, much longer.

I started off working with this 6" 1/3 HP bench grinder, but it just didn't have enough power to do the tough polishing required on a really grimy blowtorch.

Then I got this 8" 1 HP grinder, which I would now say is definitely what's required. Various buffing wheels, different polishing compounds, and different wire brushes are also required.

Keep safety in mind; I never buff or brush without leather gloves, plastic goggles, and a nose/mouth dust filter. This can be a pretty messy operation, with buffing residue ending up all over your workshop. Some have built an enclosure or a shield around the buffer area, with a shop vacuum hookup to help contain the mess.

All that protective gear is necessary when wire brushing the bronze burner and cast iron parts. Note the heavy leather gloves, dust mask over nose and mouth, eye protection with heavy plastic guard, and hat. This is a messy business.

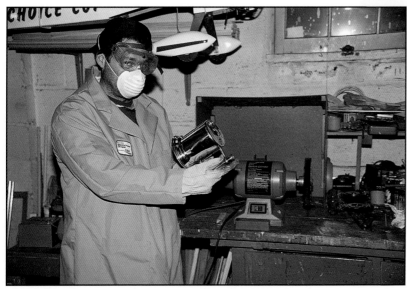

This is actually my neighbor posing for the camera, not a blowtorch collector, but he is wearing all the appropriate equipment for wire brushing and/or buffing torch parts.

The wire brush has been replaced with the buffing wheel to polish up the brass parts, and all the protective gear is still very necessary.

The burners on almost all blowtorches are made of cast bronze, and they are rough surfaced castings; you do not want to try to smooth them and buff them to a high shine. They were never like that when new; most enthusiasts agree that wire brushing the cast burners to get them clean leaves them with an attractive, as-cast appearance. A coarse, rough wire brush will do a good job, and will clean any burner, no matter how carbon covered it may be, to like-new condition. Other rough-cast parts on the torch, such as the filler plug on the bottom of the tank and the soldering iron hook, are also cleaned up by wire brushing.

The priming cups on most torches are made of cast iron, occasionally cast brass, and are held in place with a setscrew; they are also cleaned up with a wire brush, along with the steel pipe from the tank to the burner. A cast iron control knob, if used, and the steel needle valve shaft are also cleaned with the wire brush. Except for the needle valve shaft, I usually spray paint the cast iron parts with satin black or any other desired color; this improves their appearance and keeps the bare iron from rusting in the future.

Some torches are made with a steel tank, cast iron or steel priming cup, cast iron filler plug and control knob, cast iron pump top and pump handle, etc. You can remove the rust from steel and iron parts with a coarse wire brush on the bench grinder, finishing up with sandpaper in the tight spots. Try to get rid of all the rust so it won't show up later. Although the steel and iron parts may have had some other sort of finish or no finish when new, I usually prime and paint them with RustOleum spray can paint when refinishing a torch; it's easy and protects the parts. I use black, steel gray, or sometimes red or dark green for a different appearance. Occasionally you may see a brass tank with a steel lower flange pressed in place; likely done so the heavier rim will provide some extra stability. Here I buff the brass tank, wire brush the steel base flange, mask off the brass and simply paint the steel portion of the tank. Used carefully, spray can primers and color paints will provide a good looking painted finish.

Make a lamp out of a blowtorch? Sure, you can do this; I've seen many blowtorch lamps for sale in antique shops. Probably not something a real torch collector would do, but I have to admit they can make an interesting lamp. I use steel tank torches or commonly available brass torches as a base for the lamp rather than a really rare collector's item, and I don't drill holes through the tank or otherwise deface it. I usually get away with just one modification, drilling out and re-tapping the top hole where the soldering iron hook was, to accept a threaded tube which mounts the lamp socket and switch assembly. That's it; with an appropriately sized harp to take the lampshade, your blowtorch lamp is done. I've made a few painted red, orange, and purple for our grandchildren - they went over quite well as gifts.

This was a common, low cost blowtorch with a steel tank. I removed the rust and gave it a nice spray can paint job along with a Pepsi-Cola vinyl decal. The light socket was mounted by drilling out and tapping the soldering iron hook position for the lamp fitting.

The brass tanks and any other brass hardware on a blowtorch can be cleaned and buffed to a high luster. I wish there was a magic liquid that would strip off a hundred years of corrosion and dirt, but I haven't found one yet. I have heard that there are some acids that will clean up the brass, getting them to a point where they can be easily buffed. I'm simply reluctant to use any acid, even if considerably diluted, from fear of accidents. I scrub the torch with cleanser and a stiff brush to a point, occasionally using coarse steel wool, and then go to the buffer to really shine it up. I have successfully used a soft wire brush on badly corroded or stained brass, but you must be very careful not to go too heavy with the wire brush on brass or you'll put in scratches that simply won't be buffed out. A spiral sewn cotton or sisal stiff buffing wheel with the black emery compound will polish away stains and corrosion, and a loose cotton buffing wheel with white compound is used for the final buffing, also called color buffing. A buff rake is used to clean the old compound from the buffs occasionally. Parts of the torch that can't be reached with the wire brush or buffing wheels have to be done by hand, with steel wool, polish, or scraping; do the best you can.

Another note on safety here; when buffing any part of a torch, hold very tightly to it. The wheel can catch the item being buffed on occasion and will try to pull it away from you, usually throwing it down or forward.

Buffing metal is an art that can be learned with a little practice. More detailed buffing instructions are available from firms selling buffing supplies and equipment, and the Blow Torch Collectors Association can provide considerable information on cleaning and buffing torches. Some people recommend waxing the torch when you've finished polishing it; the wax will help your torch retain its shine. Some people recommend spraying the polished brass with clear lacquer to protect the shine, but I don't

do it. I don't have professional level spraying equipment, and my concern is that if the lacquer coating gets scratched, you'd have to strip the whole thing for polishing anyway.

Cleaning, polishing, and painting really make a torch look good. Hopefully, you'll find torches that are complete, with no missing parts. When parts are missing, it's nice to have "spare parts torches" on hand as a source for replacement parts. I've bought torches with badly damaged tanks, broken burners, or having some missing parts, just to use them for the parts they do have. Missing pump handles can be replaced with brass drawer pulls, available in many sizes and styles. Pump shafts can be made from brass or steel rod, cut and threaded to suit. I've replaced missing control knobs with cast iron outdoor water faucet knobs, having them welded in place. Some torches have wooden handles for adjustment rather than control knobs. Using a small lathe, I've turned wooden replacement handles from hardwood dowels fairly easily. I've made replacement soldering iron hooks, using brass rod bent into a C-shape and brazed to a cut-off brass bolt. Other repairs I've made have been to re-solder loose fittings in place, using a propane torch to do the soldering. And missing wooden handles can sometimes be replaced with wooden handles made for various tools, such as file or chisel handles. It's fun figuring out how to make the parts you might need, and while the completed torch won't be completely authentic, it'll look good.

Some members of the Blow Torch Collectors Association are reproducing a few blowtorch parts to assist the salvage of old torches, and they offer these parts for sale to other members. Available now are the small turned wooden handles used on older torches, reproduction cast brass soldering iron hooks, and even some reproduction decals for several manufacturers' models.

Several different reproduced manufacturers' decals are available now for your cleaned-up blowtorch, and more may be made in the future. Many older blowtorches have had their identifying decals lost over the years, and you can't buff up a brass tank without losing what's left of the decal.

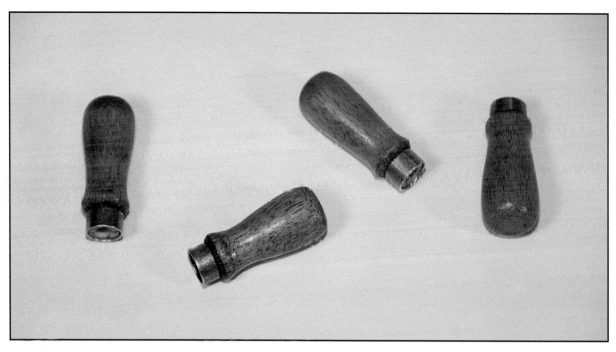

Reproduction wooden handles are also available to improve the appearance of your restored older blowtorch. The original wooden handles are frequently lost or burned by the time we find a torch to clean up.

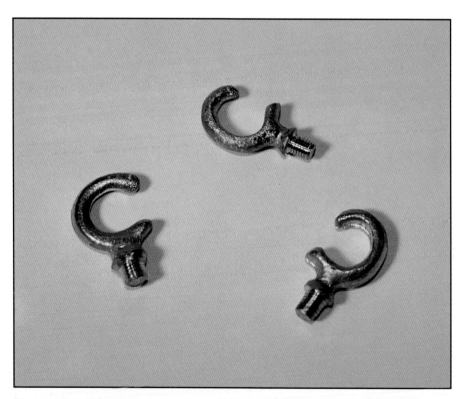

The one item most often missing on an old blowtorch is the cast brass soldering iron hook. Now a torch collector has arranged to have this item reproduced, just as they were originally made, and we can buy them for our collectors' items.

Chapter Eight
Where to Find Blowtorches, and Their Value

These days, blowtorches are generally regarded as collectible, antique items of some value, so obviously we can first expect to find them where other collectible and antique items are for sale. This means the usual antique shops and stores, antique malls, and antique and collectible flea markets. Big cities or small towns, large antique shops and malls, or small shops…I've seen blowtorches for sale in all those places - and more. Household garage sales are a possibility, but I suspect not a likely one due to the age of old torches; unless it's a garage or estate sale of an older home. I've heard that country farm sales offer a good potential that a torch or two may be among the items for sale.

Outdoor or even indoor flea markets sponsored by a local organization, newspaper, or club of some sort are, in effect, a community garage sale and you're likely to find anything there. Blowtorches are frequently grouped with other old tools, and may be considered by the seller as simply an old tool, possibly in working order, possibly not, usually not worth too much. There are shops specializing in old, used tools, and these are a good potential source for torches. In one large antique tool shop apparently specializing only in woodworking tools, when I asked about blowtorches I was taken into a back room to see three shelves filled with old torches. Antique car shows and swap meets, with their associated flea market sections offering used car parts, tools, and memorabilia are also a likely source for old blowtorches.

I've found that it pays to ask about what you're looking for; I wouldn't bother asking a dealer offering only glassware if he had any blowtorches in the back room, but in a dealer's location with a large selection of old tools or a selection of a number of older brass items, I'll tell them I have an interest in blowtorches and ask if they have any. Several times when I've seen one torch out for sale even if it's not one I want, asking about torches results in seeing several more that were in the back, out of sight.

Obviously other blowtorch collectors would be sources for trading, buying, or selling torches - but how do we find other blowtorch collectors? Reading through the classified section of one of the many antique newspapers around, I once spotted an ad asking for "old brass blowtorches, send photo, description, and price." It was the

first indication I had that there actually were other people out there interested in old blowtorches. I responded to the ad with a letter going all the way across the country, saying that while I didn't have any torches for sale, I was glad to see that someone else was collecting the same thing I was interested in. In response I received a phone call, from an ardent blowtorch collector anxious to talk to a fellow enthusiast. It turned out to be Ron Carr, and he is the individual who went on to write, edit, and publish *The Torch*, a newsletter for blowtorch collectors. Ron later founded and organized the Blow Torch Collectors Association.

Ron has run a "blowtorches wanted" ad in a number of antique papers in different sections of the country, with varying results. It seems that many of the people responding to such an ad feel that the torch they have must be worth a small fortune; a problem to any collector. I know that Lionel train and other collectors consistently advertise in local newspapers; presumably they get enough response to justify their ads. I've told family members and friends that I'm interested in and collect old blowtorches and as a result have gotten several torches as gifts, from cellar or attic clean-out sessions. It pays to advertise.

I hesitate to discuss the pricing of blowtorches, as with any collectible, you won't please everybody. Buyers want low prices, sellers want high prices. I can say that in my experience, the pricing does vary somewhat in different parts of the country but in general has been quite flat over the past ten or so years. More recently, say the past year or two, pricing has been increasing particularly for the rarer torches, due, I believe, to the advent of the Internet online auctions. We'll go into this with more detail in the next chapter. Blowtorches seem to be priced for the most part without regard for their age or rarity, which is understandable because so few people know much about them, and there has been little or nothing published on the subject. This is unfortunate, as it results in common steel-tanked torches being overpriced when they might otherwise be salable, and rare older torches going at a bargain price; good for the collector, bad for the seller. Some dealers raise the price on anything with an older patent date, which may or may not be appropriate with a blowtorch. Patent dates should not be taken as the date of manufacture;

the same patent date, say 1921, will be seen on torches produced ten or fifteen years later than that date. Many dealers base their prices on the supposed fact that anything old made of brass must be valuable.

Prices at a garage sale or flea market will be lower than in an antique shop or mall, which is reasonable as the shops have additional overhead expenses and they're in business to make a profit. Prices at an old tool shop will vary depending on whether the torch is considered a tool in good or bad condition that may or may not be usable, or an antique and therefore collectible old tool. Larger torches are generally priced higher than smaller torches, which certainly is not always appropriate. Cleaned up and highly polished blowtorches will almost always have a higher price tag because of the time and effort that has been invested, although the wrong kind of cleanup may actually lessen the collectible value. I've seen a number of blowtorches converted to lamps, usually by drilling several holes, which certainly reduces the value to a collector; but the resulting lamps have a high price. All of these pricing comments will be familiar to those who collect almost anything; as usual, the more you know about the item, whether buying or selling, the better you will be able to assess a fair and reasonable value to it.

To give some idea of the pricing you can expect to find on an average or generic blowtorch, at flea markets I've seen a range of several dollars to $25, with an average likely around $10. Antique malls and shops, $5 to $35, maybe up to $50, with an average closer to $25. For a really rare item, prices can run from $35 to $75 or more if the seller has some understanding of what he has. A few examples follow. Clayton & Lambert was probably the largest blowtorch manufacturer. A typical, common "1921 Clayton & Lambert" in any condition would usually be worth a minimum simply because there are so many of them available. The typical Lenk small torches are seen in such quantities that their price is usually, and should be, quite low. As always, a rare model Clayton & Lambert or Lenk small torch will still be at a premium. Completeness should have a big impact on the price of any particular torch, new, old, rare, or common. Missing parts should result in a lower price.

As with any collectible item, if a blowtorch is complete with its original box and/or operating instructions, its value will be higher. Very few large torches will be found with their original packaging. The smaller alcohol or two tube type torches are much more frequently found with their box and instructions, probably because it was easier to store them indoors in their original packaging. Torch manufacturers' catalogs, advertisements, product operating instructions, or any other printed matter is desirable and can be valuable, even without the torch. Collectors seek the catalogs and ads to increase their knowledge about blowtorches and to be able to more accurately date any torches they acquire. Tool catalogs, magazines with blowtorch ads, and any paperwork or printed materials pertaining to a blowtorch, are salable and collectible.

One dealer problem is that his customer base is limited to those that enter his shop - and there are not too many blowtorch collectors around to wander in and pay a high price for a rare torch. It's a case of supply vs. demand. Friendly negotiation is usually a part of the game. To the collector, if the price seems too high, don't buy it. To the seller, if it's not selling, try a lower price; if they're going fast, raise the price. Chapter 13's photo gallery and price guide will provide specific price ranges for a large variety of collectible blowtorches.

Chapter Nine
Internet On-Line Auctions

Internet-based auction sites have had a major impact on the selling and collecting of almost everything, and this certainly includes blowtorches. At this time, the largest and most successful on-line auction site is eBay, and my comments are based primarily on their operation. The numbers are impressive. Right now eBay has 2,330,103 items listed for sale, in 2,978 different categories, and one of those categories is Blowtorches. eBay gets over 1.5 billion page views per month. In 1999, eBay had 7.7 million registered users, listed 36.2 million items, and had gross merchandise sales topping $741 million.

For the blowtorch collector, a typical check of the eBay site will show approximately 50 to 75 torches listed for sale. Other sites should also be checked: blow torch, blotorch, soldering torch, soldering iron, jewelers torch, etc. Each item will be listed for about 5 to 10 days, then the auction will end. Since there are auctions ending every day, a daily check will show about 5 to 10 new torch listings. The collector can look at 50 different blowtorches for sale, with 5 to 10 new ones added every day, without leaving the comfort of his own home! If you are the successful bidder on an auction, you send your money order or check to the seller and he ships the torch to you - a pretty easy way to collect.

The on-line auctions have been particularly good for dealers and/or collectors who want to sell blowtorches. Instead of being limited to clientele who wander into a store or flea market, the items they want to sell are now available to be seen by potentially millions of people. Previously, even if a dealer knew he had a rare and/or older blowtorch and wanted to price it accordingly, unless a knowledgeable collector happened to come to his place of business there wasn't much chance of a sale. Pricing is ultimately determined by supply and demand, and with knowledgeable collectors checking eBay and bidding against each other, pricing will go up to whatever people will pay to get the item of their choice. I've seen rare torches sold for prices close to $500. Conversely, if a torch put up for sale is a common one which has been produced in large quantities and is easily available, there may be no bidders at all even at a price of $5 or $10. Condition doesn't seem to affect the price of a torch, as long as all the parts are there. A torch with missing parts is usually worth very little and would be bought only by a collector for parts use.

For collectors/buyers, the news is mixed. On-line auctions provide a large number of torches for your possible purchase. To see that many torches, you would have to go to an awful lot of flea markets or antique malls. But, if a particular torch is a highly desirable piece, a number of collectors will likely be bidding on it and the competition will result in a higher price.

I'd suggest you not get carried away and pay too much for a torch; there is a good chance you'll see another one come along later. On eBay, you can check the "completed auctions" listing and see what torches have been selling for over the past few months to get an idea of their market value. I don't think torches should be bought as an investment; you probably won't be able to sell the collection in ten years and use the profit to pay for your child's college education. Buy them and collect them for fun and your own enjoyment, and they just might go up in value as time goes by and more people learn to appreciate and desire them.

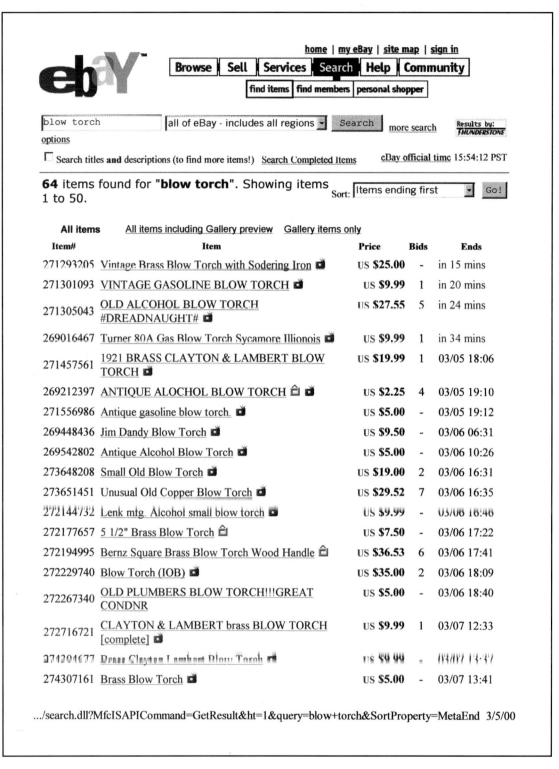

eBay™

home | my eBay | site map | sign in

Browse | Sell | Services | Search | Help | Community

find items | find members | personal shopper

| blow torch | all of eBay - includes all regions ▾ | Search | more search options | Results by: THUNDERSTONE |

☐ Search titles **and** descriptions (to find more items!) Search Completed Items   eBay official time 15:54:12 PST

64 items found for **"blow torch"**. Showing items 1 to 50.   Sort: [Items ending first ▾] [Go!]

All items   All items including Gallery preview   Gallery items only

Item#	Item	Price	Bids	Ends
271293205	Vintage Brass Blow Torch with Sodering Iron 📷	US $25.00	–	in 15 mins
271301093	VINTAGE GASOLINE BLOW TORCH 📷	US $9.99	1	in 20 mins
271305043	OLD ALCOHOL BLOW TORCH #DREADNAUGHT# 📷	US $27.55	5	in 24 mins
269016467	Turner 80A Gas Blow Torch Sycamore Illionois 📷	US $9.99	1	in 34 mins
271457561	1921 BRASS CLAYTON & LAMBERT BLOW TORCH 📷	US $19.99	1	03/05 18:06
269212397	ANTIQUE ALOCHOL BLOW TORCH 🏠 📷	US $2.25	4	03/05 19:10
271556986	Antique gasoline blow torch. 📷	US $5.00	–	03/05 19:12
269448436	Jim Dandy Blow Torch 📷	US $9.50	–	03/06 06:31
269542802	Antique Alcohol Blow Torch 📷	US $5.00	–	03/06 10:26
273648208	Small Old Blow Torch 📷	US $19.00	2	03/06 16:31
273651451	Unusual Old Copper Blow Torch 📷	US $29.52	7	03/06 16:35
272144732	Lenk mfg. Alcohol small blow torch 📷	US $9.99	–	03/06 16:46
272177657	5 1/2" Brass Blow Torch 🏠	US $7.50	–	03/06 17:22
272194995	Bernz Square Brass Blow Torch Wood Handle 🏠	US $36.53	6	03/06 17:41
272229740	Blow Torch (IOB) 📷	US $35.00	2	03/06 18:09
272267340	OLD PLUMBERS BLOW TORCH!!!GREAT CONDNR	US $5.00	–	03/06 18:40
272716721	CLAYTON & LAMBERT brass BLOW TORCH [complete] 📷	US $9.99	1	03/07 12:33
274204677	Brass Clayton Lambert Blow Torch 📷	US $9.99	–	03/07 13:37
274307161	Brass Blow Torch 📷	US $5.00	–	03/07 13:41

.../search.dll?MfcISAPICommand=GetResult&ht=1&query=blow+torch&SortProperty=MetaEnd 3/5/00

This is what you'll see on your computer screen going to the eBay on-line auction site and searching for "blowtorch." At this time there were 64 items showing up for sale, and in this section the prices ran from $2.25 to $36.53. The prices usually continue to increase right up to the ending time of the auction, and sometimes go up dramatically for a rare item. You can also search for "blow torch," "blotorch," or "soldering torch" and will see even more items for sale. It's fun, but don't get carried away.

Internet on-line auctions now make it possible for sellers to show their collectible merchandise and antiques, including blowtorches, to collectors all over the world. Blowtorch collectors likewise now have the ability to search for collectible treasures all over the world. But there will always be people out there at the farm auctions, garage sales, and flea markets searching for rare items whether the motive is profit or private collecting. That's what makes it all fun, the different ways to add to your collection. The Internet and its on-line auctions is now a big part of collecting.

One of the main tasks a blowtorch was used for was the heating of a soldering iron, to perform a variety of soldering jobs. Before electrically heated soldering irons, and electricity for that matter, were commonly available, heating the soldering iron by use of a blowtorch was the way of getting the job done. And out on a farm or a construction site, without a convenient electric outlet, the blowtorch could be used for this task. Blowtorches were also commonly called soldering torches. That's the reason for the hook on the top of most blowtorches; that hook is not to be used to hang up the torch, its purpose is to hold the soldering iron in place so the operating flame of the blowtorch can heat its copper tip.

The hook, in conjunction with a notch on the top front end of the burner casting, positions the soldering iron so that its copper block tip is right in the flame of the blowtorch. Shaped blocks of copper are used as the working end of the soldering iron because the copper will heat up rapidly, retain the heat while being used, and is easily tinned with a layer of solder to facilitate the actual soldering. Another, older name sometimes used for this tool was a soldering copper.

You can see that the hook on the top of this Clayton & Lambert blowtorch is there to hold the soldering iron in the right location so the copper tip is in the proper spot to be heated by the torch's flame. When the iron is hot enough, it is removed from the torch and used to do the soldering job at hand.

The soldering iron has three basic parts; the copper tip that actually does the work, an iron shaft which positions the copper tip, and a wooden handle so the worker can hold and use this tool. The wooden handle will not heat up; the copper tip obviously will be very hot and the iron or steel shaft will eventually be too hot to hold.

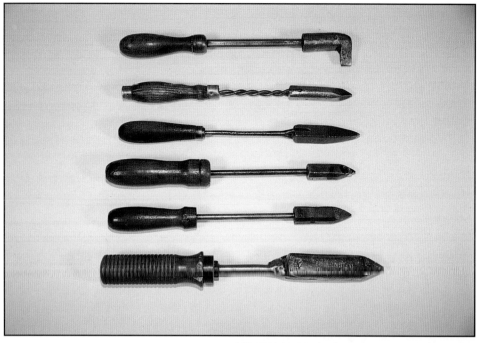

Here are six different soldering irons, they're made in different configurations and sizes for different jobs.

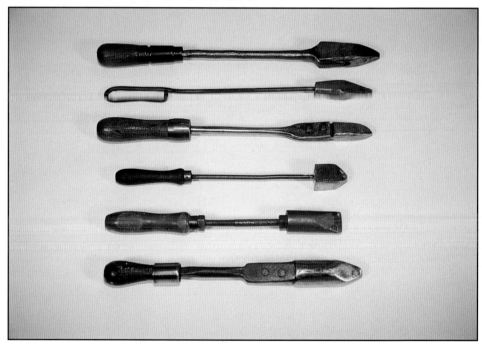

Six more soldering irons, again all different. Most blowtorch collectors include at least a few soldering irons in their collections. An iron can of course be displayed in place on a blowtorch.

As the soldering iron is a simple, robust tool, many of them have survived for 50 to 100 years and can be found today by the collector; many blowtorch collectors include at least a few soldering irons in their collection. As you might expect, soldering irons were produced in a variety of interesting configurations, shapes, and sizes; just the thing for a collector to go after. The copper tips were made in different sizes and shapes for different jobs. The iron shafts varied depending on the weight and size of the tips, and how the piece was manufactured. The wooden handles also differ in shape and size.

The soldering irons can be displayed in place on a blowtorch, selecting the appropriate iron to suit a particular blowtorch.

Soldering irons are cleaned up for display just as the blowtorches are cleaned. A wire brush wheel on a bench grinder quickly and easily takes the rust off the iron shaft and removes the carbon and corrosion from the copper tip, to make it look like new. The wooden handles can be stripped, stained, and varnished.

Soldering irons are frequently spotted at antique malls and/or flea markets, usually at reasonable prices.

Chapter Eleven

Information Sources

If you want to learn more about blowtorches, you need information, and that means paper; reading material. Blowtorches won't show up in an encyclopedia, and probably not in any library index. But there are sources; among the best sources are old catalogs, anywhere you can find them. Old tool catalogs, old Sears & Roebuck catalogs, particularly industrial supply catalogs. One catalog I've seen with a lot of good blowtorch information was a 1915 Bicycle and Motorcycle Supply book. Other good sources could be plumbers', electricians', and auto mechanics' tool catalogs.

Manufacturers' product catalogs are of course good information sources, and are sometimes available direct from the Company, if they're still in business today. I wrote to the Bernz Co., expressing an interest in their early blowtorches, and they were kind enough to send me a copy of one of their early 1900s catalogs. Antique malls frequently have a dealer specializing in publications, and they most likely will have a section on tools, a good place to look for advertisements, catalogs, etc. Old magazines can have blowtorch ads or articles about them, particularly magazines such as Popular Mechanics and *Mechanix* Illustrated.

Another interesting avenue for information is old patents. Copies of early patents are available from the U.S. Patent Office in Washington, D.C. Some technical libraries at colleges and universities have collections of patent books, and you can get access to them and have copies made. With the patent date, even just the patent year, and/or the manufacturer's name, you may be able to locate a blowtorch patent. The intricate patent drawings and frequently complex discussions of how the item works are another part of this blowtorch hobby.

Today, the Internet is of course a great information source for almost anything - but you won't find too much about collectible old blowtorches. I'll list two informative websites I am aware of, but as things change quickly on the net, I can't guarantee that this information will be current. Best thing to do is to try a search yourself. The Blow Torch Collectors Association does have a web page, www.blowtorch.net, which I believe will continue to grow and improve as an information source for us collectors. A very interesting and informative site produced by a most knowledgeable collector is "Zangobob's Blowtorch Heaven" at http://members.aol.com/blotorches/.

Having other blowtorch enthusiasts to talk to is a great way to find out more about the torches; to make that easier, join the Blow Torch Collectors' Association and you'll learn from their information resources.

Here's a Clayton & Lambert advertisement from a 1929 issue of Popular Science Monthly. I wish I could find more old ads like this one.

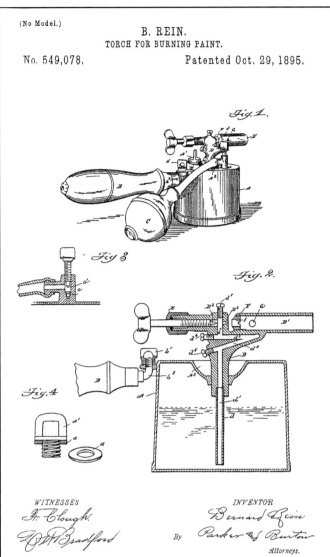

B. REIN.
TORCH FOR BURNING PAINT.

No. 549,078.   Patented Oct. 29, 1895.

Fig. 1.

Fig. 3.

Fig. 2.

Fig. 4.

WITNESSES   INVENTOR
F. Clough.   Bernard Rein
                          By   Parker and Burton
                                   Attorneys.

This 1895 patent shows the use of a rubber bulb to pressurize the fuel tank, rather than an air pump.

F. RHIND.
VAPOR BURNING LAMP.

No. 494,938.   Patented Apr. 4, 1893.

Fig. 1.

Fig. 2.

Fig. 3.

WITNESSES   INVENTOR
A. J. Tanner.   Frank Rhind
C. M. Newman.   by O. H. Hubbard
                                  his Attorney

THE NORRIS PETERS CO., PHOTO-LITHO., WASHINGTON, D. C.

In this 1893 patent, the item is identified as a vapor burning lamp rather than a blowtorch. This device does not have a pressurized tank.

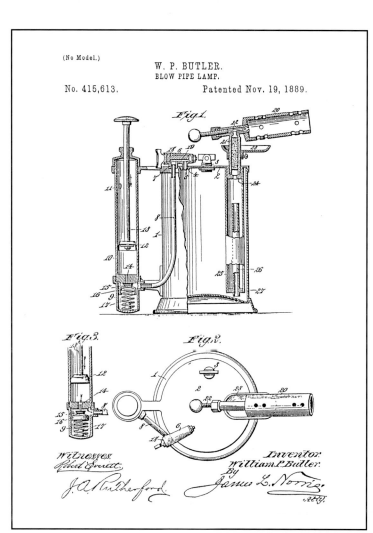

An 1889 patent for a blowtorch with the pump in the handle.

Another pump in handle type torch in this 1897 patent with a designer's different ideas.

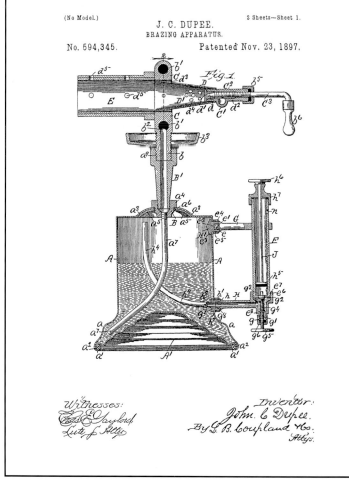

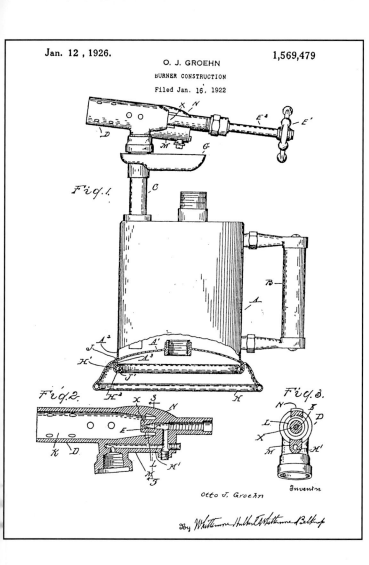

A later 1926 patent design with the pump in the tank.

Here's a blowpipe alcohol torch design in this 1899 patent.

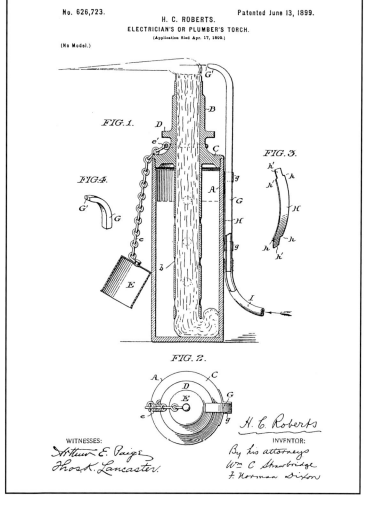

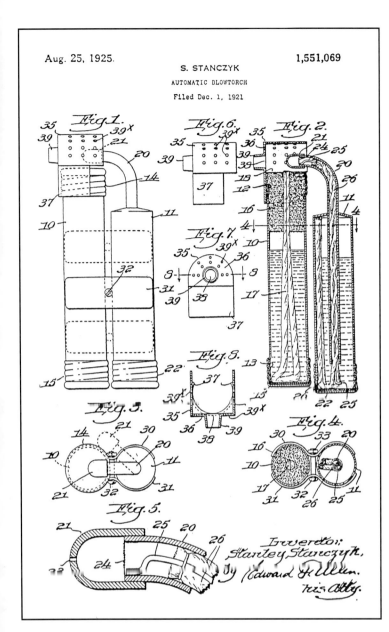

Aug. 25, 1925.

S. STANCZYK

AUTOMATIC BLOWTORCH

Filed Dec. 1, 1921

1,551,069

A 1921 patent for a two tube alcohol torch.

This Chicago Cycle Supply Co. catalog from 1915 contains a few ads for Turner blowtorches.

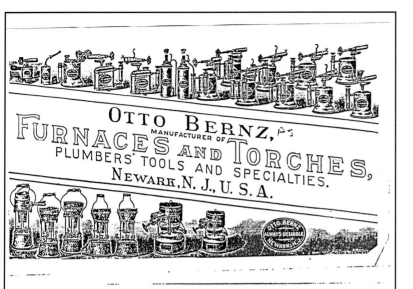

CATALOG NO. 30

3

A LL our "Always Reliable" furnaces and torches are made of the best materials obtainable. Each is carefully tested, and we guarantee to make good by repair or replacement, when delivered at our factory, transportation prepaid, any imperfection or defect in material or manufacture of such furnace or torch not caused by use, misuse or neglect, provided that all imperfect or defective parts shall be referred to us before any claim for repair or replacement shall be allowed. This guarantee continues for six months from date of sale to the purchaser either by the jobber or by ourselves.

Our furnaces and torches use less gasoline than any others on the market.

Each furnace and torch is packed in a strong box, properly labeled, and when received by you is in a condition to ship without further expense or trouble.

We also manufacture a complete line of plumbers' tools, test pumps and plugs, mercury and air gauges, pulls, sewer cleaners, etc., etc., and are always in a position to make *prompt shipments* of the above, together with our furnaces and torches which all buyers will acknowledge is a saving of time and freight.

February 1, 1916.

Yours very truly,
OTTO BERNZ.

DESTROY ALL PREVIOUS ISSUES

The Otto Bernz Catalog no. 30 from 1916 is a great help in identifying a lot of the early Bernz blowtorches.

The Bernz Catalog no. 5 has much helpful information, but we don't know what year it was issued.

CATALOGUE No. 5

OTTO BERNZ

Manufacturer of

PLUMBERS TOOLS

"ALWAYS RELIABLE"

FURNACES AND TORCHES

AND

Mechanical Specialties and Small Brass Work

OFFICE AND WORKS
21-43 South 13th St., near South Orange Ave.
NEWARK, N. J.

E S T A B L I S H E D   1 8 7 6

This Turner Brass Works Catalog of 1915
describes many of the early Turner blowtorches.

This catalog sheet of a French blowtorch
manufacturer in 1912 would be even
more interesting if I could read French.

Opposite page:
This Swedish torch manufacturer's sheet
from the 1950s is printed in Spanish, but
it's still interesting.

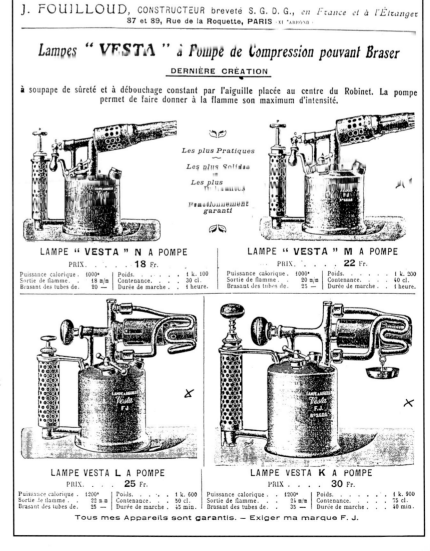

SIEVERT 257
Sin "Quickstart"

FORMADOR DE LLAMA
No. 9953 para llama plana

SIEVERT 'QUICKSTART'
acorta el tiempo de encendido de la lámpara a 1/5 del normal

SIEVERT 257T
Con "Quickstart"

LAMPARAS DE SOLDAR
PARA GASOLINA

Este tipo de lámpara combina el buen funcionamiento de la antigua lámpara de gasificador en espiral con las exigencias actuales de limpieza automática de la boquilla y fácil limpieza de los canales de gasificación. La llama se regula con una rueda manual y el quemador tiene una pantalla contra el viento con soporte para soldador. El depósito es de latón con el fondo doble emballetado y soldadura dura; la bomba con válvula que se puede cambiar fácilmente y tapón de llenado con válvula de seguridad. Con cada lámpara se entregan juntas de repuesto.

SIEVERT "QUICKSTART"

Las lámparas de soldar SIEVERT 251—269 pueden también entregarse con un encendedor rápido Sievert "Quickstart". El tiempo de encendido para una lámpara de, por ejemplo, 1 litro se acorta entonces a menos de un minuto. El encendedor arde con el mismo combustible de la lámpara — sin alcohol.

Datos de capacidad, consumo, peso, etc.									
Modelo sin "Quickstart" .... Sievert No.	251 Gesek	252* Getta	257 Gesju	258* Gerde	259* Germa	263 Geott	264* Getro	268 Gebin	269* Genlo
Modelo con "Quickstart" .... Sievert No.	251T Geten	252T* Gelle	257T Geslo	258T* Genta	259T* Genor	263T Gelar	264T* Genbe	268T Geldi	269T* Genas
Capacidad del depósito .... litros	0,8	1,0	1,0	1,6	2,0	2,0	3,0	3,0	4,0
Llenado normal .... litros	0,65	0,90	0,90	1,45	1,85	1,85	2,70	2,70	3,70
Consumo por hora a presión normal .... litros	0,75	0,75	1,4	1,4	1,4	2,5	2,5	3,2	3,2
Consumo máximo a mayor presión .... litros	1,7	1,7	2,7	2,7	2,7	4,7	4,7	6,15	6,15
Longitud de la llama ...... mm	275	275	400	400	400	450	450	550	550
Diámetro de la boca del tubo de llama .... mm	19	19	27	27	27	34	34	42	42
Distancia del fondo al centro del tubo de llama .... mm	200	210	220	250	272	276	320	330	400
Altura total .... mm	230	240	250	280	320	320	365	380	450
Diámetro del fondo del depósito .... mm	105	119	119	132	132	132	146	146	146
Peso sin "Quickstart", exclusive embalaje .... kg	1,38	1,75	1,87	2,23	2,43	2,64	3,52	3,84	4,27
Peso con "Quickstart", exclusive embalaje .... kg	1,45	1,76	1,96	2,31	2,51	2,71	3,60	3,92	4,35

The best thing you can do if you have an interest in anything collectible is to join the national organization for people with the same interest, if there is such an organization. We're in luck, as there is a Blow Torch Collectors' Association. It's an informal thing, and does not have elected officials, rules, etc. It does have a great newsletter, *The Torch*, which is published about four times a year, and contains a wealth of information of interest to torch collectors. Ron Carr, as the founder of the BTCA, has amassed quite a collection of torch information that he shares with his fellow enthusiasts.

The Newsletter has articles on torch cleaning and restoration, descriptions of particular torches, information on torch manufacturers, stories about members' activities, travels, torch acquisitions, etc. With members in other countries, there is even information on foreign blowtorches and collecting. The other members' names are available, so you can get in touch with other collectors in your area. Copies of blowtorch patents are periodically included in the Newsletter. Specific torch questions can be directed to the BTCA and among their collective membership you will most likely get the answer.

The Newsletter even contains a For Sale or Trade section, to facilitate selling and trading between members. And contributions come to the Newsletter from members all over the world, recounting their own torch collecting experiences. Members have supplied copies of patents, catalogs, blowtorch instruction sheets, manufacturers' literature, etc., so that others may learn more about these fascinating devices.

The BTCA has held, so far, two Annual Conventions for their members; both were held in the Seattle Washington area. Plans are to continue with a yearly convention, possibly in different parts of the country each year. Those attending bring as many blowtorches as they can from their collections, for the fun of displaying them and possibly for sale or trade with other members. Such gatherings are expected to grow in size and in activities as the BTCA continues to attract new members.

For information on the BTCA and to join, contact:
Ron Carr
3328 258th Ave., SE
Issaquah, WA 98029-9173

And check out the BTCA web page at www. blowtorch.net

The patch of the BTCA, available to members.

Blow Torch Collector's Association

Ronald M. Carr, President, Editor The Torch

Phillip C. Anderson, Editor The On-line Torch

3328 258th Ave. SE

Issaquah, WA 98029-9173

The Blow Torch Collector's Association, BTCA, is a relatively young group that came together in early 1995 with a goal of preserving the history of blow torches, promoteing collecting knowledge, and the trading or selling of torches within the group. BTCA has over 110 members to date and cover 32 states as well as members in Canada, Australia, N. Ireland, England, Tanzania, Sweden, and France to add an international flavor. As with any organization or antique group, BTCA members come from all walks of life, with torch collections that number from a few torches, up to a record 3000, with 75 -150 being the average.

~Ron Carr

Microsoft is a registered trademark and the Microsoft Internet Explorer Logo is a trademark of Microsoft.

Click Here to Email B.T.C.A

This is the Internet home page for the Blow Torch Collectors Association. Check it out.

67

The BTCA has held several Annual Conventions for its members. Here is John Dorffeld with his display of blowtorches and soldering irons.

Maurice Jernstedt with the blowtorches he brought to the Convention.

Mark and Arlene Pederson with some of their blowtorches collected over the years.

Larry Fields, at the Convention with some of his torches.

BTCA member Phil Roach with a selection from his torch collection.

They even had a blowtorch cake at the Convention.

The display of Les Adams, a BTCA member who came over from his native England for the Convention.

A very interesting display of rare and old blowtorches by Ron Carr.

Chapter Thirteen

Photo Gallery and Price Guide

The best way to learn more about blowtorches is to see as many of them as you can. To help you do that, I've included pictures of as many torches as I could in this section, with as much information as possible about each one of them. I'm always learning more about blowtorches as additional old catalogs, advertisements, patents, etc., become available either through other collectors, the Blow Torch Collectors Association, or material I'm able to find through the usual antique/collectibles sources. There will be photos included here of blowtorches that I've just been unable to identify and don't know much about; but that's part of the fun of collecting. Perhaps collectors out there who read this book will provide more information to me about some of these torches; I'd appreciate that.

Many of the torches pictured are shown after a considerable effort has gone into their disassembly, cleaning, and polishing. This was done not with any thought of actually operating them, as I believe that would definitely be too dangerous to consider and would require careful repair work be done. I feel these torches look so good when cleaned and polished that is the only way I will display them. Many collectors prefer to do a minimum of cleaning and maintain their collected torches in an as found condition. For this reason and because I haven't cleaned and polished all the torches in my collection, many of the items pictured are in as found condition.

Along with the photos is my best effort at a usable price guide. The price ranges shown are based on ten years of blowtorch collecting experience, with time spent at shops and flea markets in many parts of the country, from New Jersey to California. I've also utilized inputs and advice from other collectors across the country. Even so, please realize that these prices are intended as a guide and that there are many variables which will affect the price of a collectible blowtorch. The prices shown are based on a totally complete torch, no missing parts, in reasonable condition. Scratches, fairly small dents, and very minor repairs do not seem to affect the price. Missing parts and major damage can and should be reflected by a considerably lower price. You can't go to the local hardware store these days to replace a pump, soldering iron hook, priming pan, or control knob on an old blowtorch.

Rarity along with age has the biggest effect on the pricing of a torch. Common, easy to find old blowtorches bring a minimum price. Blowtorches from the late 1800s and early 1900s, particularly seldom seen models, bring top dollar among collectors. Whether it's a common gasoline blowtorch or a miniature alcohol type, rarity is the key to its value. Some manufacturers produced a very large number of torches, with so many surviving and available today, that they simply aren't worth much to the collectors. You can't always trust the seller's sales pitch; because a blowtorch is described as old, unusual, rare, and valuable doesn't mean it's true, only that the particular seller feels his item has those attributes. And, up to now, blowtorches have generally been accorded one basic price range in most antiques and collectibles guides, typically $35 for a small torch and $75 for a larger one. This simply isn't the case in the real world, and as awareness of the intricacies of blowtorch collecting grows, the pricing will become more realistic. I hope this book will help.

As covered in Chapter 9, Internet on-line auctions have greatly affected the pricing of most collectibles including of course blowtorches. When hundreds and thousands of potential collectors can view a particular blowtorch up for sale and be bidding against fellow collectors, you can usually count on the price going up if it is a rare item. It has happened a number of times that with a very desirable and rare blowtorch up on an on-line auction, the competitive bidding has gotten the price up to $500 or more. Likewise, with a number of the same torches available on an on-line auction, some won't get any buyers even at a $5 or $10 selling price. You can still get what I'd consider a bargain, even in an on-line auction. Again, it depends on who's watching at a particular time and who recognizes how rare or unusual an item may be. Different collectors look for different things. Even with a reasonable price estimate for an individual blowtorch, an on-line auction may result in a much higher or much lower realized sale price.

The photo gallery will be organized into these arbitrary groupings: Conventional Pump-in-Tank Blowtorches, Pump-in-Handle Torches, Pint Size Blowtorches, Torches Without Pumps, Auto Torches, Foreign Torches, Mini

Torches including Two Tube, Blow Pipe, and Jewelers' Torches, and Miscellaneous Types/Unusual Torches.

I believe this price guide information will be of assistance to both collectors and sellers, but please remember it is at best a guide. Supply and demand in the marketplace along with a good understanding of the rarity, age, and condition of the particular piece will always determine the final price for a collectible blowtorch. Good luck.

Section 1. Pump-in-Tank Blowtorches

This Clayton & Lambert model 308 has a 1921 patent date and a more complex burner assembly than most blowtorches; it was made in the 1930s. The lower control valve is there only to admit fuel into the priming cup, making it easier to pre-heat the burner before lighting off the torch. $20-$45.

Nice chrome plating makes this an attractive blowtorch, featuring a separate control valve to admit fuel into a priming cup for pre-heating before lighting. Manufacturer unknown. $20-$45.

This Sears Craftsman blowtorch has a comfortable molded pistol grip handle for easy use. $5-$25.

A very early Clayton & Lambert blowtorch, model 2, with a 1902 patent date. The burner does not have a soldering iron hook, and the attractive handle is made of intricately shaped brass. $20-$50.

This Bernz blowtorch made in 1951 is one of the very few torches ever made with an aluminum tank, making it a nice addition to any collection. Also a very nicely shaped tank. $15-$50.

Bernz blowtorch with a particularly nicely shaped tank. Bernz also made a limited number of torches with this same shape, but of aluminum rather than brass. $10-$40.

A Wall blowtorch with low cost steel tank construction; almost no brass is used in this torch. $5-$15.

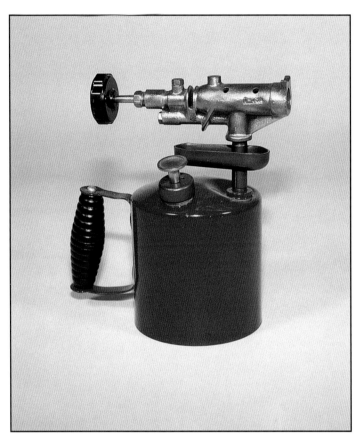

Turner T-15A from the 1960s, a very low cost blowtorch with simple construction and a steel tank. $5-$10.

A Wall blowtorch with low cost steel tank construction and Wall's unique cast iron burner assembly. Wall was the only torch manufacturer to use a cast iron burner rather than bronze, and they used this iron burner on a number of different style blowtorches. $10-$25.

Wall blowtorch with a steel tank, their unique cast iron burner, and the pump location in the tank at an angle above the handle. $10-$30.

Wall blowtorch with a different handle and pump construction. Handle is steel, brazed to the steel tank and pump housing, which exits the tank at an angle above the handle. $20-$50.

This low cost steel tanked Turner T-15C was made in the 1960s, one of the last blowtorches to be manufactured. $5-$15.

This Bernz blowtorch is made with a steel tank. Most Bernz torches were made with brass tanks, but they also made lower cost economy models like this one. $5-$20.

This steel tanked Turner offered the convenience of a separate control valve to admit fuel to the priming cup for pre-heating the burner. $5-$20.

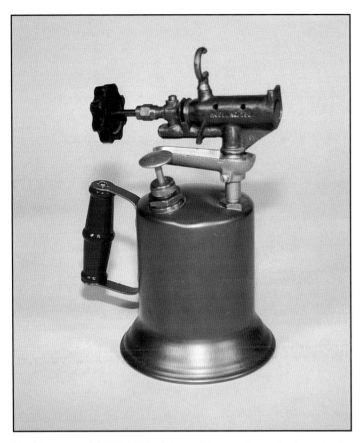

The Turner model 150 still had the well-known Turner trademark of an acrobat on a bar on the pump handle. $5-$15.

Made by Unique, this blowtorch looks similar those of other manufacturers, but differs in the details of its tank shape, handle attachment, pump, and burner design. $10-$25.

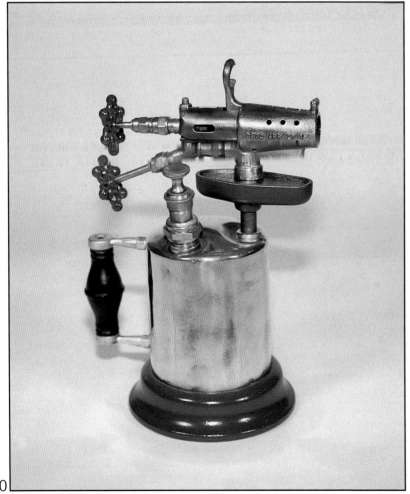

This Clayton & Lambert model 208 blowtorch with its 1915 patent date has some very interesting features. The tank is brass, but the lower base on the tank is steel, and the handle standoffs are made of aluminum. The soldering iron hook is part of the burner casting, and that burner features their double control needle arrangement. $20-$50.

A Clayton & Lambert model 600A with a 1921 patent date, a pretty generic example of the type, produced in the 1940s. $10-$25.

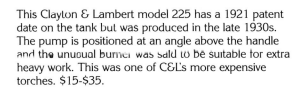
This Clayton & Lambert model 225 has a 1921 patent date on the tank but was produced in the late 1930s. The pump is positioned at an angle above the handle and the unusual burner was said to be suitable for extra heavy work. This was one of C&L's more expensive torches. $15-$35.

Clayton & Lambert model 144A from the 1940s. $10-$25.

Turner model 206A from the 1930s. $10-$25.

Nice looking blowtorch, appears to be a Turner but no identifying marks. Manufacturer unknown. $10-$20.

Nice Bernz blowtorch, probably from the 1940s. $10-$30.

Manufacturer unknown, estimate 1950s. $5-$25.

Pistol grip, chrome plated blowtorch, interesting burner, no identifying marks. I believe this was made by Bernz, likely as a subcontractor to another firm. $15-$35.

A Hauck blowtorch, very interesting features, and not often seen. Likely from the 1920s or 30s. $25-$50.

A large gallon size blowtorch, by Bernz. The gallon size torches are very rarely found today. $25-$65.

A large and heavy gallon size blowtorch by Hauck, very interesting. $25-$75.

A Turner gallon size blowtorch. Standard burner, pump, and handle, all on the very large tank, not often seen. $25-$65.

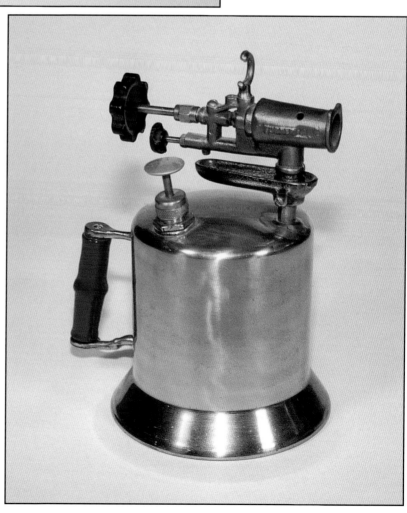

A Turner Double Jet blowtorch with the pump in the tank. Haven't been able to identify the specific model, but estimate it's from the 1920s. $35-$75.

Clayton & Lambert, probably a model 208 variation, this blowtorch has a 1915 patent date on the burner. Has a dual control valve design, advertised as the greatest general utility quart torch made. $15-$40.

This blowtorch by the Geo. W. Diener Mfg. Company is marked as a No. 2 and has a very interesting handle. The handle may look like the typical wooden type, but it is actually made of coiled steel wire. This is the only Diener torch I have seen with a pump in the tank. $25-$50.

Clayton & Lambert model 32A blow-torch, built in the 1930s. $10-$30.

Clayton & Lambert model 32 blowtorch, with a cast-in soldering iron hook. This particular example has a brass tank with a steel lower flange around the tank. $20-$45.

Clayton & Lambert model 144 blowtorch, made in the 1920s. $15-$35.

Clayton & Lambert model 327 blowtorch, advertised as their heavy-duty torch, made in the 1950s. $15-$35.

Clayton & Lambert model 158 blowtorch, made in the 1930s. $15-$35.

This steel tanked torch has a somewhat different burner design, and was made by the Unique Mfg. Co., Chicago, IL. $10-$30.

Clayton & Lambert model 800 blowtorch, from the 1950s. $10-$30.

Although this blowtorch has no identifying marks, its design characteristics show it to be a Schaeffer & Beyer. $15-$45.

The label on this blowtorch says Hercules Guaranteed Torches, but I suspect it was manufactured by Turner. $10-$25.

Although there is a Turner trademark on the pump handle of this blowtorch, the burner says M.W. & Co. Special. Likely put together from parts of two torches. $10-$20.

This blowtorch is nicely identified as a product of the Detroit Torch & Mfg. Co. $10-$30.

This blowtorch is labeled Champion Quality Products, but was apparently made for them by the Turner company. $10-$45.

This blowtorch is a Preway, produced by the Prentiss-Wabers Products Co. of Wisconsin Rapids, Wisconsin. $20-$40.

Turner blowtorch, model 206A1. $10-$25.

A Bernz blowtorch, probably from the 1940s or 1950s. $10-$25.

This very heavy Bernz blowtorch has a large, complex burner and a brass handle with removable cap that contains a tool to clean the burner orifice. $20-$45.

A Bernz blowtorch, probably from the 1930s or 1940s. $10-$25.

This blowtorch is quite standard in appearance, but has the manufacturer's name, Butler, cast into the burner. It's the only torch I've run across with this name. $20-$40.

This very low selling price steel tanked Dunlap was made by Turner and is basically their model T-15A, but with a pistol grip. $5-$15.

93

This Detroit Torch & Mfg. Co. model has a most unusual burner assembly with a cast bronze main section and a cast iron top piece, providing a narrow rectangular opening for the flame. Also has interesting wound wire control knob and wound wire handle. $125-?

Rarely seen is a blowtorch by this manufacturer, the A.E. Lovett Co. of East Orange, New Jersey. The burner is vertical, with a screwdriver adjustment rather than a control knob. The brass tank is copper plated. $75-$150.

The maker of this blowtorch is unknown. It has an unusual pre-heater fitting with a separate fuel feed pipe out the top of the tank. IL13 is stamped on the pre-heater casting. Any blowtorch with unusual features is a bit more desirable. $35-$65.

This blowtorch is identified by the Welch, Chicago cast into the burner. This burner and pre-heat bowl are obviously designed for use in a vertical position, but on this example the burner is mounted horizontally and with a conventional pre-heat pan. $35-$65.

This blowtorch with interesting construction and features is particularly large and heavy. It's made by Hauck, Brooklyn New York, and is their No. 15. $40.-$80.

Section 2. Pump-in-Handle Blowtorches

Turner Double Jet blowtorch, model no. 96 from the 1910s, has an unusual and interesting burner design and pump in the handle. $30-$75.

Turner Double Jet blowtorch, estimated to be from the 1920s, very interesting burner assembly. $30-$75.

Turner Double Jet blowtorch, likely from the 1910s, with a unique pivoting arrangement on the feed line to permit relocating the burner assembly to a variety of positions. $40-$125.

Nice older model by the Detroit Torch & Mfg. Co. with a patent date of 1918. It has a stamped steel bolt-on soldering iron hook. $20-$50.

Quite rare Vesuvius no. 36 blowtorch by the American Stove Co., St. Louis, Missouri. The steel tank on this torch was originally copper plated, but the plating was lost during clean-up, so I painted the tank. $25-$75.

Older blowtorch by the Schaefer & Beyer Co., Newark, New Jersey. The Otto Bernz Co. was also located in Newark, and many of the Schaefer & Beyer and Bernz torches resembled each other greatly and had similar design features. $20-$55.

This old Clayton & Lambert model no. 108 was made in the 1920s and while this example has a broken soldering iron hook and a split in the tank, it's still a nice addition to a collection. $20-$50.

An Ashton model 43 blowtorch. The Ashton Mfg. Co. was also located in Newark, New Jersey, along with the Schaeffer & Beyer and Bernz companies. Ashton's trademark was their Red Hot brand name. $20-$55.

This is a Torrid model blowtorch by the George W. Diener Mfg. Co., Chicago, IL. It was most likely made in the 1920s. $20-$55.

This Ashton Red Hot blowtorch has a patent date of 1902; it's a very early torch, and has a cast-in soldering iron hook as part of the burner. $20-$60.

This Ashton blowtorch has a patent date of 1902, and a unique burner design with the pre-heating vein going around the burner. An unusual and rare find. $30-$85.

Although this very interesting blowtorch has no identifying marks, judging by some of the design characteristics I'd guess it was made by the George W. Diener company, likely in the 1910s or 1920s. $20-$55.

This blowtorch is an M.W. Special, with an interesting control knob and priming cup. It's nice to see a torch by a lesser-known manufacturer. $20-$50.

An old Bernz model 57 blowtorch from the 1910s, with a nice wire wound control knob. $20-$60.

An old Turner-White no. 13 Hot Blast blowtorch from the 1910s. $20-$60.

A most unusual configuration, this steel tanked blowtorch has the pump in the handle, pointing upward. No identifying marks, but judging by the burner style I believe it was made by the Everhot Mfg. Company. $25-$85.

Turner Master Line Baffle Model no. 45, from the 1920s. A very interesting configuration, with the pump mounted horizontally and the handle mounted vertically, to the pump. Neat cast brass control knob. Fairly rare. $20-$65.

A Bernz blowtorch, likely from the 1920s, with a clamp-on soldering iron hook. $20-$50.

A Bernz blowtorch with a cast-in soldering iron hook and a 1910 patent date. $20-$50.

This blowtorch has no identifying marks, but by its design characteristics I'm sure it was made by Schaeffer & Beyer. $20-$50.

This blowtorch with a 1910 patent date was made by the Detroit Torch & Mfg. Co. It has no provision for holding a soldering iron. $20-$50.

Old and very dirty, this Clayton & Lambert blowtorch is probably from the 1910s and will take a lot of work to clean and polish. $20-$50.

Nice example of a White/Turner Hot Blast blowtorch, although a corner of the pump handle is broken off. It's interesting that the top of the pump and the pump handle are cast iron rather than brass. $20-$50.

This old blowtorch unfortunately is made up of an Ashton Red Hot tank and a Turner burner assembly. I'll save it for spare parts. $15-$35.

The burner on this older Bernz blowtorch is a very clean design, although the torch was most likely made in the 1910s. $25-$55.

This older Shapleigh Hardware Co. blowtorch, probably made by a large manufacturer for the Shapleigh label, has a particularly attractive stamped brass diamond shape identification plate on the tank. $40-$75.

This older blowtorch by the Globe Light and Heat Co., Chicago Illinois, has a tank made up of three pieces and an air line from the bottom of the pump to the top of the fuel tank, an unusual arrangement. Quite a rare and valuable torch, likely made around 1900. $125-?

This blowtorch is a Turner No. 21, made in the 1910s. $20-$55.

Nice Bernz pint size blowtorch has the pump in the tank but uses brass tube handle in brackets designed for a pump; may have been made this way to use up existing parts. $15-$45.

A Clayton & Lambert model 160 from the 1930s. Nice details include cast brass handle brackets. $20-$50.

This Bernz pint size blowtorch has a soldering iron hook and complex brass casting handle brackets, likely made in the 1920s. $20-$50.

This early Turner torch, likely from the 1930s, has three identifying numbers on it; 159, 136, and 105. Details like this make it difficult to positively identify a blowtorch model. Nice cast brass control knob and ribbed wood handle. $20-$50.

Low cost steel tanked Clayton & Lambert, likely from the 1950s. $5-$20.

This pint size Turner from the 1920s has a chrome plated finish on the brass tank, not frequently seen. $20-$50.

Very interesting Clayton & Lambert pint size blowtorch with a 1902 patent date, probably a model no. 9, has a mix of features. Brass tank, steel lower flange around the tank, machined aluminum handle standoffs, soldering iron hook cast as part of the burner. An unusual specimen. $25-$60.

A rare and unique Turner Double Jet Blow Pipe No. 8 pint size from the 1910s. Nickel-plated brass construction, with the ability to tilt the burner head to various positions. $30-$85.

Unusual blowtorch by the Welch company, Chicago, with feed tube, burner, and priming cup specially designed for vertical operation. $25-$65.

Nice early Turner Hot Blast no. 315 blowtorch from the 1910s. $30-$85.

Unique configuration pint size blowtorch by the Ridgely Trimmer Co. of Springfield Ohio. Soldering iron rest is on the top of the pump handle, and the control knob works via a right angle drive arrangement. This torch design was patented in 1912. $30-$85.

Very early Clayton & Lambert pint size blowtorch with a 1902 patent date and additional valve control on the bottom of the pump. $25-$55.

111

Early Clayton & Lambert model no. 19
blowtorch with a 1902 patent date. $20-$55.

Schaeffer & Beyer blowtorch, almost identical
to the blowtorch below left, but this torch has
the fuel feed exiting near the edge of the tank.
$25-$60.

This early Schaefer & Beyer pint size blowtorch has
a 1912 patent date, a formed steel soldering iron
hook that bolts in place around the burner, and a
pump handle that screws down on the pump to
hold it in place. The fuel feed tube exits in the
middle of the tank; later models had the tube
exiting near the edge of the tank. $25-$60.

A very early pint size Bernz blowtorch with a 1909
patent date, and no soldering iron hook. $20-$50.

Left:
This pint size blowtorch by the Detroit Torch & Mfg. Co. has a 1909 patent date. $20-$50.

A pint size Ashton Red Hot blowtorch. $20-$50.

Right:
This pint size Turner blowtorch has two identifying numbers, 136 and 106, making it hard to positively identify the model. Likely made in the 1920s. $20-$45.

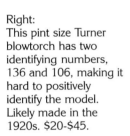

This very early pint size blowtorch is by one of the lesser-known manufacturers, Baum & Bender of Jersey City, New Jersey, probably from the early 1900s. Nice to see some of the more rare models. $35-$65.

A pint size Clayton & Lambert torch with a 1921 patent date on the tank and a 1924 patent date on the burner. Damage to the end of the burner and pump handle replaced with a tire valve will lower the value of this piece. $10-$25.

113

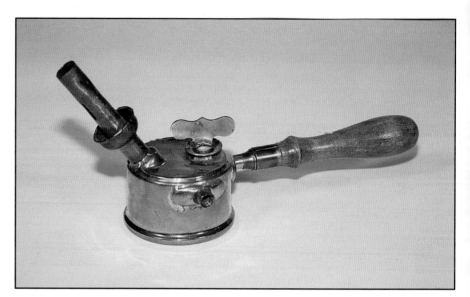

This Vulcan blowtorch, by Bernz, with its 1893 patent date, is one of the very earliest torches known. Had two mounting positions for the handle, a priming cup around the burner tube, filler plug, and no pressure pump. Extremely rare. $75-?

This Clayton & Lambert No. 8 blowtorch appears in their 1910 catalog. The tank is a brass casting, and there are two mounting positions for the handle. A pre-heating cup is machined into the top of the tank. A Bernz catalog around the same time had an illustration for a No. 8 torch that appeared virtually identical to the C&L No. 8 torch. By either manufacturer, this is a very old and rare model. $75-?

A very early Bernz blowtorch with a 1910 patent date. The cast bronze tank is extremely heavy. Torches like this are considered interesting and rare. $75-?

A National Safety Device Co. blowtorch, with patents having been issued in 1939. This particular version was likely a prototype or early production model, with later models having a handle bracket that clamped around the top section of the tank. $35-$75.

National Safety Device Co. No. 200 blowtorch, this example with a chrome-plated finish on the brass tank. $30-$70.

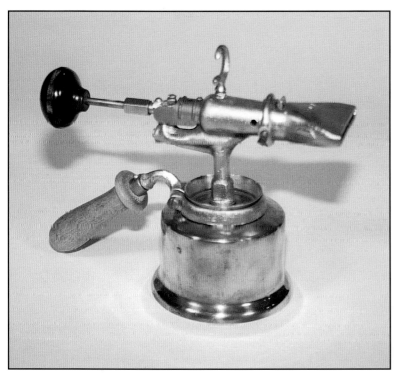

I believe this is the National Safety Device Co. No. 200 Pumpless Safety Blowtorch, produced in the 1940s. This example has the wind shield in place, along with the flame spreader attachment. $35-$75.

This Coleman blowtorch has an unusual configuration, with the burner and the handle above the fuel tank. It may be a fake, never produced by Coleman, but it's still a worthwhile addition to a collection. $20-$40.

Clayton & Lambert no. 48 auto torch, from the 1920s. Narrow, for working around cramped spaces in an automobile, this early torch had a wooden control handle and a cast-in soldering iron hook. $35-$75.

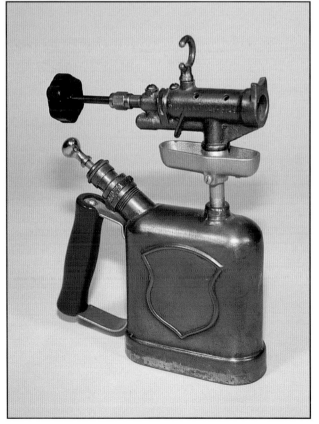

Everyone likes the distinctively shaped steel tank on this Unique auto torch. Fairly rare and a desired piece. $25-$65.

Clayton & Lambert no. 252 auto torch, from the 1930s. Pump at an angle above the handle, shield shape formed into tank. $30-$70.

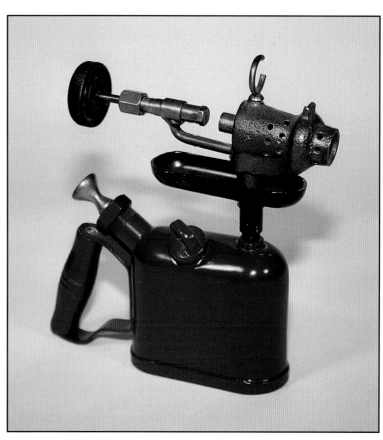

Rugged auto torch by Bernz, has pump mounted at an angle above the handle, a feature also used by other manufacturers. $30-$70.

A Wall auto torch, with their exclusive and unusual cast iron burner assembly. $25-$65.

Bernz auto torch, model no. 5, from the 1910s. $35-$75.

A Wall auto torch, with a pistol grip handle and the more conventional cast bronze burner. $20-$40.

An unusual Wall auto type torch, pistol grip handle, and a burner positioned low and at right angles to the tank. Apparently for some unknown special purpose use. $30-$50.

Below:
Extremely rare Phoenix auto torch by the Decker Mfg. Co. of Newark, New Jersey. One of very few blowtorches ever made with an aluminum tank, this one is an aluminum casting. $125-?

This older auto torch has no identifying marks, but by design characteristics I'd say it was made by the George W. Diener Mfg. Company. $30-$70.

White Hot Blast auto torch by the Turner Brass Works, from the 1910s, has a neat wound wire control knob. $30-$70.

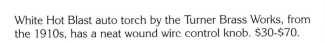

Turner's New Line auto torch with a 1920 patent date, nice cast brass control knob. $40-$85.

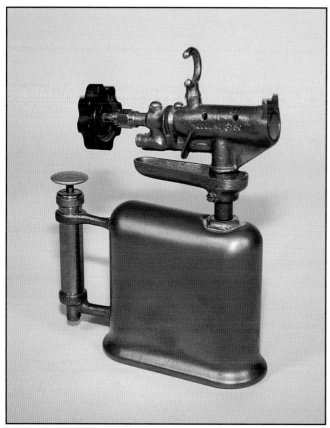

Turner model 318C auto torch, a lower cost unit with a steel tank, from the 1940s. $25-$40.

Another Wall auto torch, with a cast bronze burner and a conventional handle. $25-$40.

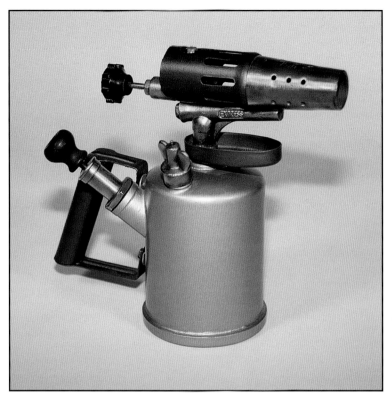

This is an Express model no. 352T blowtorch, made in France in the 1940s. Pump is in an interesting position, at an angle beside the handle. $25-$65.

This is a Swedish blowtorch, made by the Max Sievert company in Stockholm. This older model does not have a pressure pump. $25-$55.

A Rippes no. 1 blowtorch, French, made between 1935 and 1950. No pump in this torch. $25-$55.

A larger Max Sievert blowtorch, from Sweden, with the pump in the handle. $30-$60.

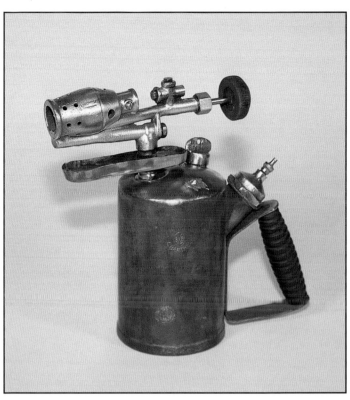

A German blowtorch, made by the G. Barthel company. The handle has a storage compartment inside, for a cleaning tool. $25-$55.

A standard size blowtorch by G. Barthel, Germany, this example has an identification plate soldered on the tank reading "Globe Gas Light Co., Boston, Mass." $35-$65.

This larger-than-usual blowtorch is a Bronzit by G. Barthel, Germany. The pump is mounted at an angle above the wooden handle. The larger torches are usually more expensive. $40-$70.

This Vesta type K blowtorch was made in Paris, France, between 1920 and 1934. Very interesting, with its perforated metal cover over the pump/handle and the formed steel fuel line around the brass burner for fuel pre-heating. $30-$70.

This is a Governor blowtorch, made in England between 1936 and 1950. Pump is in the tank, and shaped steel is used for the handle and burner supporting bracket. $25-$55.

Small blowtorch by Max Sievert, Sweden, nice looking with the pump in the handle. $25-$55.

A small Monitor no. 132 blowtorch, made in England. $25-$55.

A Radius no. 52 torch, made in Sweden. The steel parts were very badly corroded on this example, but it cleaned up nicely for display. $25-$55.

An English blowtorch, made by Chas. Twigg & Co. Ltd., Birmingham. $25-$55.

This is a Swedish blowtorch by Max Sievert, a model no. 251, produced between 1950 and 1960. It will look even better when cleaned and polished. $25-$55.

A French blowtorch, a Vesta model N, manufactured around 1939. $25-$55.

A French Vesta type E, made around 1939. Most of the foreign blowtorches have metal handles, usually steel, as compared to the wooden handles commonly used in the US. $25-$55.

This is a Burmos blowtorch, from England. $25-$55.

This is a Coleman blowtorch, made in Canada by Butler Stampings and Machine Screws Ltd. $10-$30.

A French Express no. 11 blowtorch, made in the 1950s. $25-$55.

Another Swedish blowtorch, a Max Sievert type A1 made in the 1930s. $25-$55.

Section 7. Mini Torches, including Two Tube, Blow Pipe, and Jewelers' Torches

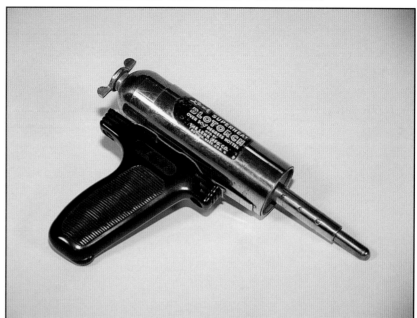

Lenk no. 222 Superheat Blotorch, uses alcohol as the fuel, intended for household use; soldering, etc. Bakelite pistol grip handle, probably made in the 1950s. $20-$50.

Lenk no. 99 Alcohol Blotorch, an earlier example of the pistol grip type of soldering torch, with a painted wooden handle. $20-$60.

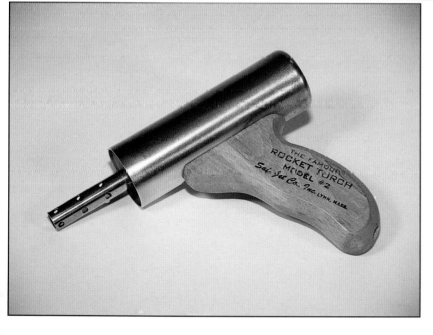

Rocket Torch model no. 2 by the Saf-Jet Co., Lynn, Massachusetts. $20-$50.

An interesting design variation, Lenk made a much smaller number of their little blowtorches using an elongated cast priming cup, like this one, in place of their standard round stamped brass cup. This style is seen much less often today. $5-$25.

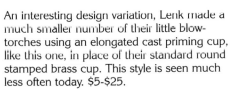

The Lenk Mfg. Co. of Boston, Massachusetts, made a wide variety of small blowtorches similar to this example, in models for alcohol and others for gasoline use. This particular one has a 5" high tank. $5-$20.

In addition to polished brass and chrome finishes, Lenk painted some of their models with a gold colored paint, like this example. $5-$20.

This small Lenk blowtorch has a chrome plated finish on its brass tank. $5-$20.

This is one of the larger Lenk models, made with a 6" tall tank. $5-$20.

An extremely rare blowtorch is this small Lenk model with a pressure pump/handle and larger burner tube. I was aware they made a model like this, and looked for ten years to find one. I've yet to see another. $50-$125.

Other manufacturers also made small sized blowtorches; this example is by Dunlap. $5-$20.

This small blowtorch with its interesting steel wind shield and soldering iron hook was made by Turner. $5-$20.

I haven't seen many miniature blowtorches by foreign manufacturers; this one is by G. Barthel in Germany. The torch is held with the burner tube vertical for pre-heating and lighting. $10-$35.

A small blowtorch made by Fulton. While it's nice to find a torch in good condition with the manufacturer's decal still there, like this one. Most of the time the brass tanks are corroded to the point that a serious polishing is necessary, and any decals left are lost in the process. $5-$20.

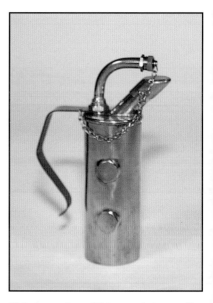

This type of small blowtorch is usually referred to as a jewelers' torch, and again the Lenk Mfg. Co. made a variety of different models. $10-$30.

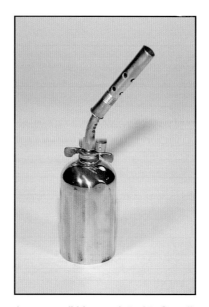

A very small blowtorch is this Scovill Imp; tank is only 3" high and less than 2" in diameter. $10-$35.

A nice collector's find is this small blow-torch by the Scovill Mfg. Co. of Waterbury Connecticut. Interesting lower brace around the tank for the handle. $10-$30.

This Lenk model has a chrome plated tank finish and only one fuel compartment. $10-$30.

Quite complex construction on this Duplex torch with a 1920 patent date, by the Peerblow Mfg. Co., Leetsdale, Pennsylvania. $10-$35.

Right:
Another Lenk model, with easy to remove filler caps on the tank. $10-$30.

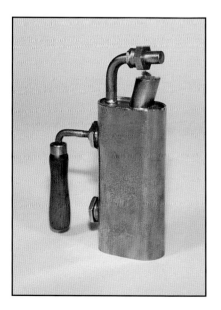

This interesting blowtorch is a Jim Dandy with a 1928 patent date, by the Lasher-Weeber Co. $15-$40.

This very small item, only 1" diameter and 6" long, is labeled as a Besjet Alcohol Blowtorch, by the Harmic Mfg. Co. of Somerville, Massachusetts. $10-$25.

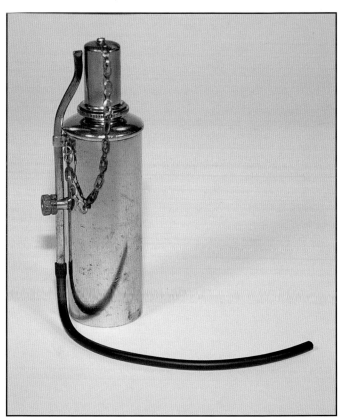

A blow pipe is designed to position an air nozzle at a right angle to the flame produced by an alcohol torch. By blowing air through a rubber tube connected to the nozzle, an intense flame can be directed and controlled to some extent by the operator blowing through the tube. Manufacturer of this example unknown. $10-$30.

This blow pipe, or alcohol torch, was made by the Victor Co. $10 $30.

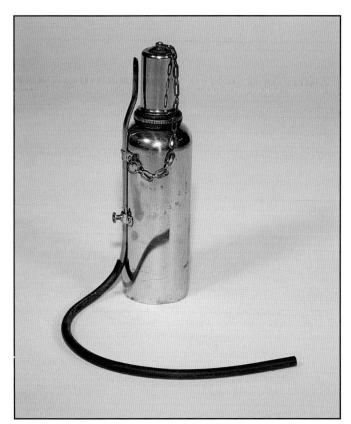

This is a nickel-plated Spartan blow pipe, manufactured by the Carlton Company of Boston, Massachusetts. $10-$30.

Nice looking copper plated blow pipe by Lenk. $10-$30.

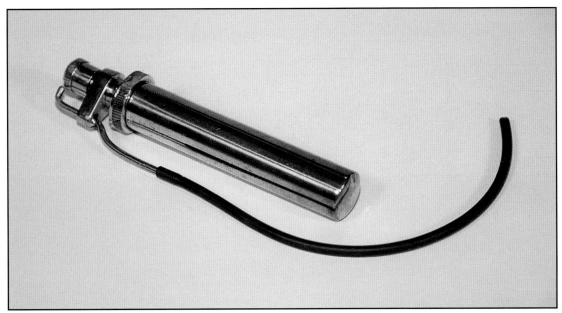

This all brass very small blow pipe was made by Bernz, and is listed in their 1916 catalog as a no. 11 alcohol torch. $15-$45.

An unusual small copper plated steel blow pipe, the No. 20 Soldering Torch, by the W.B. Marvin Mfg. Co., Urbana, Ohio. No identifying marks. $35-$75.

Larger than most self-generating alcohol torches, also referred to as two tube types, is this example by Dunlap, made by the Modern Metal Products Co., Cambridge, Massachusetts. Patented around 1934. $5-$25.

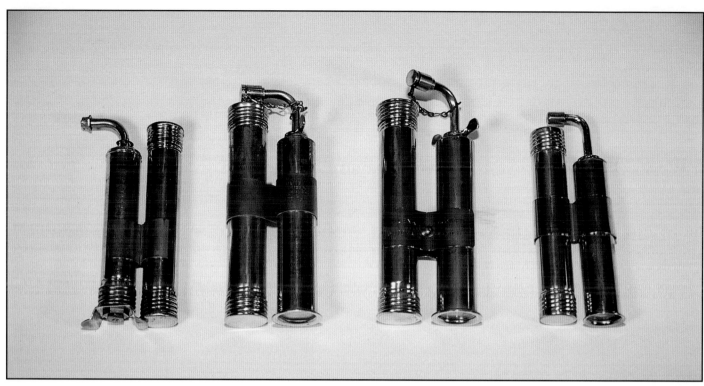

These four two tube alcohol torches are typical of those manufactured by Lenk, Jim Dandy, Dunlap, and others. $5-$20.

This two-tube device is called the Super 2000 Automatic Blow Lamp, and was made in England by Valtock and sold in the U.S. by Brookstone. $5-$25.

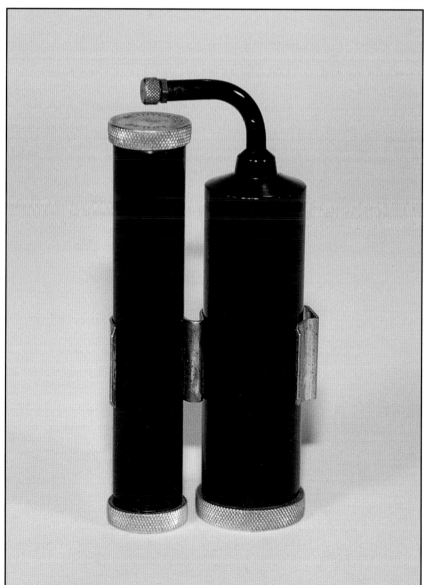

The Spitfire A-100 two tube alcohol torch, made by Robert L. Livingston, Williamsport, Pennsylvania. Features a flint lighter mounted on the pre-heat fuel tube and a red composite insulating material on the fuel tank/handle. $5-$25.

This alcohol torch by the Hanau Engineering Company Inc. was used by dentists. Pulling the trigger on the handle pumped a stream of air through the alcohol flame, directing the heat for work on dentures, crowns, molds, etc. $15-$35.

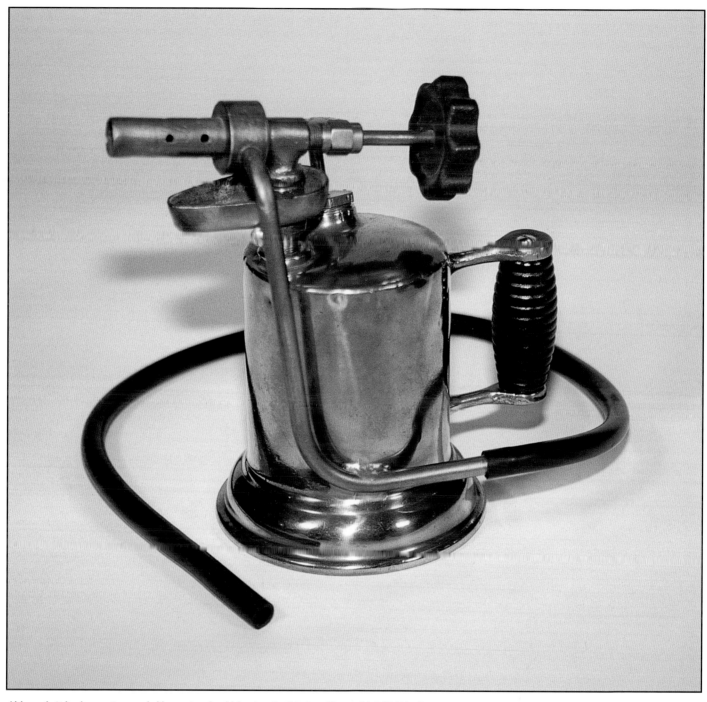

Although it looks pretty much like a standard blowtorch, this is a Turner H-1 Halide Detector. Developed around 1939, this item detects leaks in refrigeration systems. By holding the end of the rubber hose near any pipeline joints being checked, with the torch burning, if any refrigerant gas is leaking it will go through the hose and the torch's burning flame will change color. $35-$85.

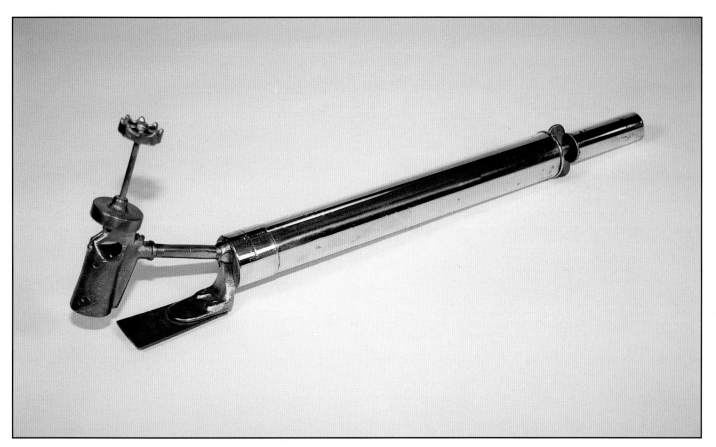

With an 1898 patent date, this combination blowtorch and paint scraper by the Climax Co., Hyannis, Massachu-setts, is a rare item highly desired by blowtorch collectors. The pressure pump handle is at the end of the fuel tank, and when held properly with the burner vertical, the priming cup can be used to pre-heat the burner. $175-?

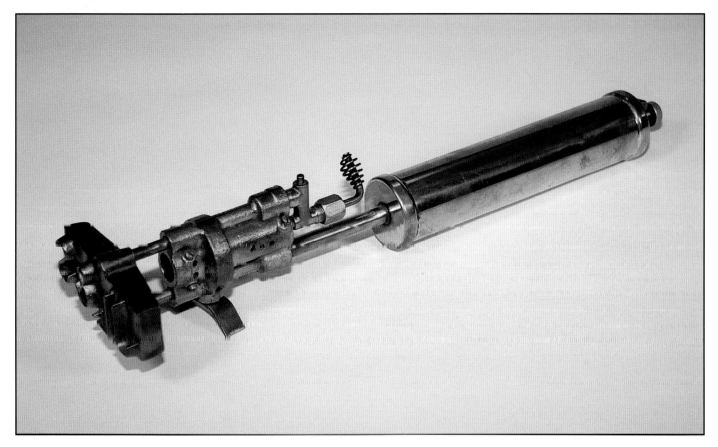

This is a self-heating branding iron, by the Everhot Mfg. Co. of Maywood Illinois. It works just like a standard blowtorch, with the pressure pump on the end of the fuel tank that serves as a handle, and the blowtorch flame heats up the branding iron. A soldering iron tip can be exchanged for the branding iron, if desired. $65-$150.

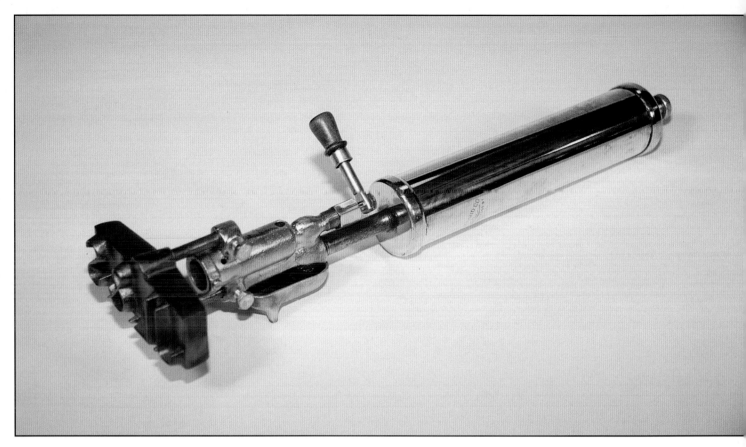

Another self-heating branding iron, this one by the Burning Brand
Co., Chicago, Illinois. These are quite rare items. $65-$150.

This is a self-heating soldering iron, by Primus, a Norwegian company. The copper
soldering iron tip is held in position ahead of the blowtorch's flame to be heated, and
the soldering tip could be removed for other uses of the blowtorch. $65-$150.

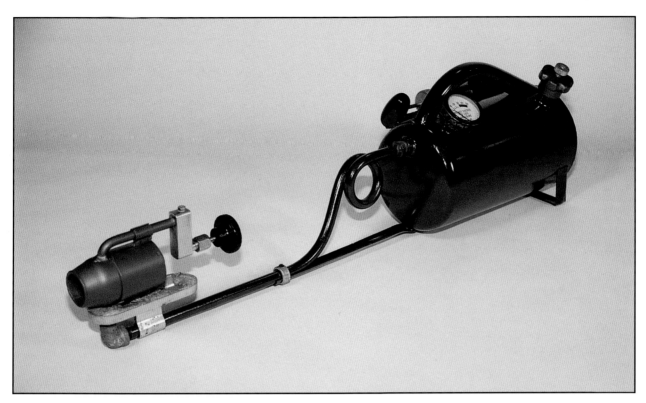

This large blowtorch is 30" long, and the tank probably holds several quarts. It's used to burn off unwanted ground vegetation on farms or in forest fire fighting situations, or even to melt ice in the winter. $25-$75.

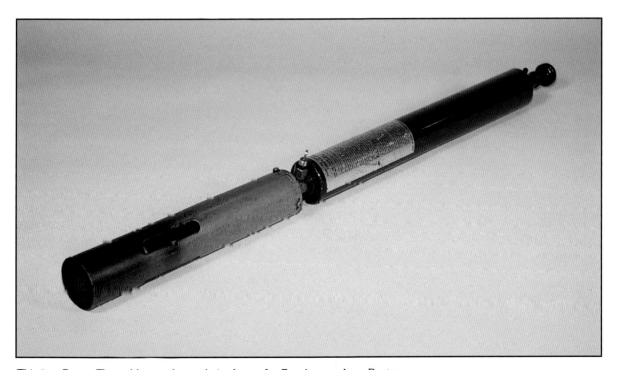

This is a Power-Flame blowtorch, made in Japan for Bandwagon Inc., Boston, Massachusetts, for burning off ground vegetation or melting ice. $20-$60.

This military blowtorch was made in the 1960s by the Hunter Mfg. Co. of Solon, Ohio. It's one of the very, very few blowtorches ever made with an aluminum fuel tank. $25-$75.

This item is not a blowtorch, it's a pressure oiler or sprayer. Such devices were made by several blowtorch manufacturers, using the basic torch tank, handle, and pressure pump along with some sort of nozzle and trigger mechanism to permit spraying some kind of liquid. You see them occasionally today, almost always incorrectly advertised as a blowtorch. This example was made by the Huffman Mfg. Co. of Dayton, Ohio. $20-$50.

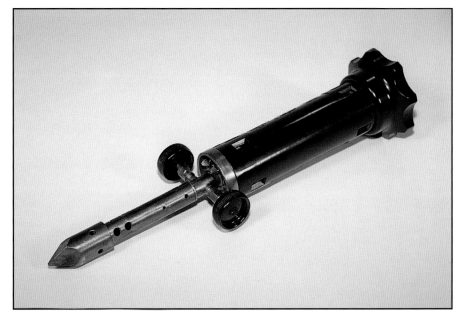

A self-heating soldering iron, this Justrite model no. 59 was made by the Justrite Mfg. Co. of Chicago, IL, and was patented in 1924. It operated on the usual blowtorch principles, and the brass fuel tank is enclosed by a Bakelite cover which serves as the handle. Soldering tips were available in a variety of types, or could be removed for other blowtorch tasks. $20-$60.

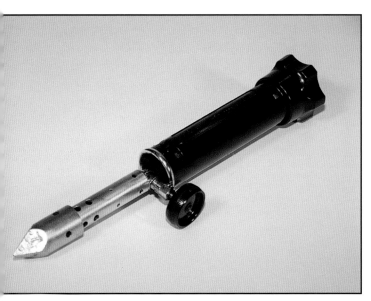

This Justrite model no. 39 was also patented in 1924. A smaller version of the Justrite no. 59, it operated in the same manner. $20-$50.

An even smaller version of the Justrite self-heating soldering iron, a small blowtorch. $20-$50.

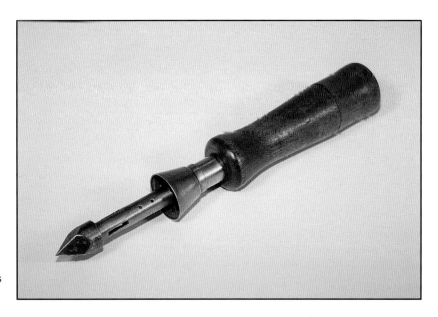

This wooden handled self-heating soldering iron/blowtorch is a Stayhot Model B, by the Thermo-Gas Products Co. The end of the wooden handle unscrews for access to the internal brass fuel tank. $20-$50.

Also not a real blowtorch, this is a miniature pencil sharpener, styled as a blowtorch. Of interest to some blowtorch collectors. $5-$15.

This is not a real blowtorch, but a battery powered, butane fueled cigarette lighter, styled as a blowtorch. May be of interest to some blowtorch collectors. $5-$25.

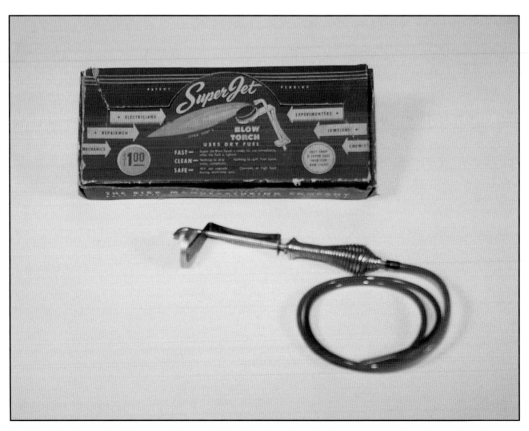

It's labeled a Super Jet Blowtorch, by the Birk Mfg. Co., East Hartford, Connecticut, but it doesn't use alcohol or gasoline as the fuel. The Super Jet burns a solid fuel pellet, and the operator blows air via the plastic tubing through the flame to direct it toward his work. $20-$40.

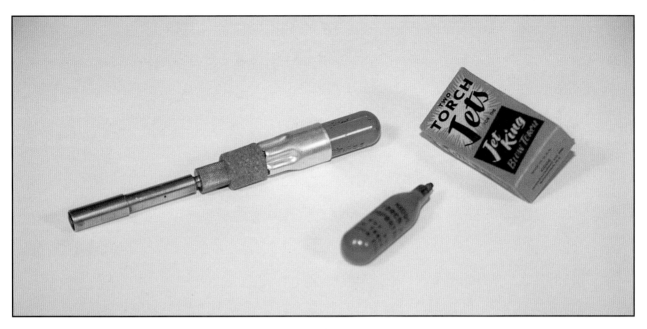

A small pencil type soldering torch, the Jet King Blowtorch by the
Kidde Mfg. Co. uses butane cartridges for fuel. $15-$35.

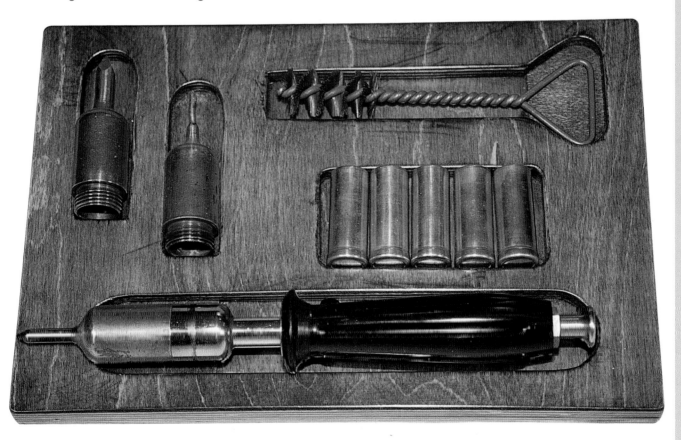

A self-heating soldering iron, identified only by Clark 1007, this military tool has interchangeable soldering tips
and is fueled by a combustible cartridge. The cartridge is inserted in the soldering iron, and a firing pin is pulled
on the end of the handle to ignite the cartridge. Soldering can be done as long as the cartridge burns. $15-$40.

Above and right: This is the oldest blowtorch in my collection, with a patent date of 1890. This torch was made by the Union Heater Supply Co. of Detroit Michigan. It came with a rubber squeeze bulb to pressurize the tank, and this example also has a tank-mounted pressure pump, which was most likely added later. This torch was listed in one tool catalog as the Favorite Paint Burner. $250-?

144